Men I Have Painted

JOHN MCLURE HAMILTON

1921

TABLE OF CONTENTS

FOREWORD

IT were well could one of the "Men I have painted" take up the pen and contribute a character sketch of the "Man who has painted me": for among all these living and admirable studies, it is doubtful if there is one individuality more unusual or more interesting than that of the writer himself. To me, the lucky chance (if anything in this world is chance) that brought John McLure Hamilton to my Hawarden home in the early 'nineties was invaluable, for it was the beginning of a deeply valued friendship, of an intercourse rich in experience. Had I the pen of a De Morgan, let alone the tongue of men and angels, a book might have been written on the five (in their different ways) unique members of this family, a book which would have surpassed even Joseph Vance or Alice for Short. May I hope to have the chance in another world.

I can never forget the moment when Mr. Hamilton, after a day or two spent anonymously in the Temple of Peace (Hawarden Castle), came into the library and asked us to come and look at his picture. I must first explain that Mr. Gladstone had a habit of concentration, acquired by long years of self-discipline, that resulted in complete ignorance of the presence of others, were they strangers or friends, in his room. So long as they read or worked in silence, his absorption would make him totally unaware of their presence.

To the immortal "Signor" (George Frederick Watts) he sat, in Little Holland House, no less than forty times, for a portrait that the artist eventually destroyed. This tragic experience had led to the determination, on Mr. Gladstone's part, never to sit to an artist again. From this time forward the only chance given was for the unfortunate man to steal silently into the room and work, as best he could, from what he saw—Mr. Gladstone at his writing-table bending over his papers, or seated in his armchair absorbed in his book. The last adventure we had had with a painter, who seemed glad to come under these conditions, resulted in a fancy portrait. Instead of painting what he saw, he placed Mr. G. in heroic attitude, standing on the terrace of the House of Commons, gazing over the river! With this absurd picture in my mind, we followed Mr. Hamilton into the Temple of Peace—literally with our hearts in our boots. The very first glance at the famous portrait (now in the Luxembourg) was arresting and delightful. For there was the man exactly as we knew him—exactly as day after day we saw him. He sat in the corner of the window, his customary place, the light that fell on his book reflected back on his face. Here was no fancy picture, but one of familiar everyday use—precious for all time, for us and for those that come after us, the man as he actually was—intent—unconscious.

Only last year I was reminded of the episode. Lord Halifax was sitting for his portrait. Mr. Hamilton had just left the house; the picture was brought to Lord Halifax. He gazed at it. "Why, it's me!" he said, intense astonishment in his voice.

When Olive Schreiner, aged seventeen, wrote the South African Farm, some among her friends were disappointed she had not called more upon her imagination and described wild and thrilling adventures, as her country might have suggested. "Such works," she says in her Preface to this wonderful book, "are best written in Piccadilly or the Strand; there the gifts of creative imagination, untrammelled by contact with fact, may spread their wings. Those brilliant phases and shapes are not for her to portray. Sadly she must squeeze the colour from her brush. She must paint what lies before her." These words might have been written by Mr. Hamilton. He is intensely real. He is a true impressionist. He paints what he sees, and as he sees it, and not as he imagines it. He paints the real, though the ideal may unwittingly be sometimes included. It is the same with his book. I have only heard fragments of it, but enough to show me its chief characteristic. It bears the hall-mark of reality, of sincerity, of truth. The book is alive—it will live.

I feel it a privilege to have been asked to contribute this word.

MARY DREW.
Hawarden, 1921.

MY FATHER

AMONG all the men I have known intimately, my father stands out as a positive, straightforward, and inflexible nature. I owe him not only my life but the manner of my life, for it was he who inclined the tree by studying the bent of the twig. Against opposition, mostly silent I imagine, for he was self-willed and determined, he not only encouraged but guided me in the direction of my tastes, placing me, at an early age, under the care of the painter, George W. Holmes, where I met Henry Thouron.

My father's love of Art was innate, but whence derived is not evident, unless two or three drawings in pencil by his cousin, Alexander Hall Hall, are evidence of artistic talent in his mother's family. From what I have heard I am led to believe that this particular Hall Hall was a dilettante who passed most of his life in Rome, content to admire Art, without seriously pursuing it. With this exception, there is no trace of either talent or taste for Art in the Hamiltons or Hall Halls, who lived in the north of Ireland prior to the trouble of '98, and afterwards in Canada and in Pennsylvania. What pictures there may have been in Tully Hall, Betty Hall's house, near Ballymena, were probably disposed of to help defray the expenses of the family's migration to America. I may have derived from my French ancestry, the Delaplaines, through my mother, some of that love for Art which survives in the old Latin civilizations.

My father's early professional life was spent among the picturesque hills and valleys of northern Delaware, where he dashed along the by-roads on his fast pacing ponies, from village to village, from farm-house to farm-house, healing the sick and comforting the sorrowing, day and night, in summer's heat and winter's cold, the counterpart of many a country doctor who sacrifices himself to relieve suffering, generously, uncomplaining, and usually but poorly rewarded.

But my father had his reward. Nature had enriched him with many gifts—a strong and active physique, a mind open to any and every simple pleasure and joy that a bountiful Providence could offer, and above all, and greatest of all, a rare appreciation of beauty. Nothing escaped his observant eye, as his horse bore him along in swift stride over hill and dale; the purple shadows of snow-white clouds passing over fields of golden corn, a blue-bird flickering into a cherry-tree in bloom, a daisy here, a violet there—all that Nature possessed, both great and small, he gathered into the storehouse of his memory, where he kept them unfaded, to recall at his pleasure. And in that place, at that time, nearly one hundred years ago, Nature was rich in the small things she cultivates for her adornment.

From the first an ardent botanist, the young doctor found a fertile field for study; and much of his time was given to the collection of flora he had commenced, when a student of medicine, on the banks of the Wissahickon. And so his mind grew in the love of beauty. Nature here inspired him, schooled him with loving care, as a preparation for his future devotion to Art.

But what contrasts his life presented! In the hot summers, battling with disease and pain in close and fetid rooms, beneath roofs on which a sun blazed with such intense fury during the day that the dews of night never cooled them, or in winter fording the Brandywine and Red Clay Creeks on horseback, through snow and ice, through hail and blinding sleet and rushing winds, he rode to save a woman's life.

And then the scene changes to long streets of bricks and mortar and white marble steps, at that time relieved by rows of maple-trees, whose pretty leaves cast their flickering shadows on the hot brick sidewalks and streets paved in cobble-stones. Here, in the old Quaker City, he began, so far as his limited resources would permit, to collect books and engravings, to gratify his taste for music and the theatre, and to frequent the exhibitions of pictures, chiefly of the Barbizon School, for there were then, in the city, several patrons of modern Art. Daubigny was one of his great favourites, and side by side were examples of Corot, Diaz, Jean François Millet, Boldini, and Alfred Stevens.

But, as I have said, books became his great hobby, and his library grew, from day to day, to the alarm of my mother, who, in the end, had to care for the thousands for which there were no shelves or cases, and find places to stow them away under the beds and chairs, or packed in high columns two or three deep, against the walls of the unoccupied rooms. I can remember one room, where I have sometimes slept, having a path only from the door to the bed, between walls of musty volumes—a disposition of books that reminds me of John G. Johnson's method of disposing of his surplus masterpieces of ancient Art in closets, bathrooms, and under the beds of his house in South Broad Street.

These books were not rare first editions or in tooled bindings that the

Grolier Club would have cherished, for the collector had no means for such luxuries; but although the paper may not have been so thick or so fine, or the edges gilt, the printed word was there, and the reader could walk in Greece with Homer, in Rome with Tacitus and Cæsar, in Florence with Dante, in France with Montaigne and Racine and Molière, in England with Chaucer and Shakespeare, and in Germany with Goethe, and commune with them as intimately and freely in humble dress as in fête-day finery. The possession of a few rare books by the great authors would have had all the advantages, without the drawbacks, of the many; but collecting for its own sake was part of the attraction. No sale of books at Thomas and Sons' auction rooms, in South Fourth Street, was ever missed; and here my father came into intercourse with men of like tastes, and competed with them for the possession of coveted volumes. The fascinating habit grew until at last no available space for more volumes could be found.

When the opportunity presented itself, he increased his collection of engravings, contenting himself with prints and proofs after letters of examples of the masters of the engravers' art—Wille, Edelinck, Audran, and Drevet—whose reproductions of the portraits of the period surpass the original paintings.

His love of Art was deeper and greater far than my own, and I may also say blinder, for study and a wider experience made me conscious and critical of defects, or, more accurately speaking, intolerant of all but the highest and noblest, while his more catholic tastes, led somewhat by his books, accepted Art in general as the one thing to be admired. Had he been wealthy, he would have been a princely patron of every form of Art.

And to this affection for the beautiful, this love of il pane degli spiriti gentili, I owe the supreme happiness of my life. Without his encouragement and assistance I might have been a slave of one of the professions—a slave as he was, in a sense, to duty. To be as free as I have been is rare, and I have gloried in freedom.

He was conservative to the backbone. He lived in the past and in the present, and he based his conduct and his thought upon the best traditions that he could find in literature. He believed in manhood, in womanhood, in childhood, and in Godhood; in patience and good-will, in faith and charity. An uppermost thought in his mind was "Will my neighbour be hurt by this, my act?" As a citizen he was loyal to the right, and intolerant of wrong. He had no doubt at all about what was right and what was wrong; that had been determined long ago by the sages. He was no friend of "progress," often miscalled nowadays, for he knew that human nature was deep-rooted, and could not be uprooted by visionaries and demagogues.

He was a strange man, very impressionable, with prejudices—but his prejudices were confined to Art and literature, never directed against people. Rachel, the great tragédienne, once visited Philadelphia, appearing at the Walnut Street Theatre. My father found her acting so perfect that he never went to the theatre again, for fear that the impression he had received might be effaced.

He was an unusually sane and just man. After Art he loved horses, and they returned his affection. He petted, coaxed, and teased them, and when in the country often groomed them himself, winning them by the choicest clumps of clover he could find, and by his manner, that was both firm and fond. Like all tactful men, he was extremely sensitive to every touch of nature, and would respond willingly to the call of both pleasure and pain—to enjoy the one and relieve the other—but he had too much faith to resent the will of God in misfortune.

The day I last saw him is recalled over the years with constantly increasing frequency as I approach the time when I too must say good-bye to the charm of earthly beauty. He came to stay at a cottage I had taken, on that delightful plateau above the Delaware Water Gap, at Swiftwater. The trees had changed their dull-green summer dress for a score of gay vestures, each one surpassing the other in richness, and under the soft radiance of an early autumn sun the mountain-sides seemed to be carpeted in fantastic designs. We drove down the valleys and up the hills through the maze of colour, our admiration increasing at every turn, until the enthusiasm of my father became so great that he rose from his seat and stood in the carriage, in order to enjoy more actively the entrancing panorama moving around us. I gazed at him with delight—it was a joy to know that neither length of years nor the deeps of sorrow had dulled one string of a mind attuned to beauty.

THE KING

A SHORT time before the coronation of King George V an idea was conceived by Mr. Donald, of the Daily Chronicle, that the members of the Senefelder Club, of which Mr. Joseph Pennell was the president, could take part in the celebration of that event by making a series of lithographs commemorative of some of the incidents connected with it. Mr. Jackson was selected to make a drawing of the Queen, and I of the King.

After some negotiations with the chamberlain, sittings were agreed to, and I received a note from Sir William Carrington to call at Buckingham Palace. I found Sir William in his very simply furnished office on the ground floor, where he instructed me how to proceed when His Majesty made an appointment. In due course the command came to attend at the Palace at eleven o'clock one morning. Sir William received me smilingly, and said, "I will conduct you to the room where you will work. The King may come in before noon. You should address him as 'Your Majesty' and see to it that you do not detain him more than twenty minutes, the time allowed"; and, as a final admonition, "Do not talk politics to him."

I was then left alone in a large central room on the second floor in the centre of the Palace and overlooking the avenue leading to Trafalgar Square. Immediately in front was the Memorial to Queen Victoria, by Brock. As the King did not come, I passed a few minutes sketching the view from the window looking down towards the Admiralty Arch in Trafalgar Square.

Some time before, I had witnessed the King proceeding in State to open Parliament from the platform of this monument, at the base of the Queen Victoria throne, and looked down upon the coach and horses as the King drove by, and upon the magnificent military guard and the vast concourse of people stretching along the avenues in all directions and over the grass of the Green Park. No better position for seeing this display of pomp and power could be imagined, and it was one of my lucky moments when I met the sculptor at the entrance door of the temporary studio that had been erected around the monument, and received a kind invitation for myself and Mrs. Hamilton to a place on the elevated platform. Few people realize how beautiful London is, but fewer still obtain the opportunity for observing from points of vantage the pageants and spectacles for which the great city forms so perfect a setting. I had time to reflect upon the spectacular character of life, and the peculiar part it plays in the economy of a nation, while I waited for the King to come. Presently Sir William Carrington returned to tell me that His Majesty had been called unexpectedly to a council meeting, and would not sit until after lunch; that I must have some, and he had ordered it up, so that I might be on hand should the King come in by chance. I told him I did not require lunch, and should work better without it. To this he hardly listened, hurrying away to his duties.

Time had fled rapidly—it was long after one o'clock, as I could see by the clock on the mantel, the clock that was to be almost my undoing a little later. Suddenly the two doors flew open with a whirr and two very tall men entered bearing trays which they put down on a table at the back of the room. The men must have been six feet three or four inches in height, and were resplendent in richly coloured liveries that shone like plush. They wore powdered hair, and silk stockings displayed well-shaped calves and ankles. Quickly placing the dishes in order on the table with a "Your luncheon is served, Sir," they silently and swiftly left me, bewildered by the unexpected splendour of their appearance. Had I rubbed Aladdin's lamp the genii could not have been more prompt in carrying out an order.

On the table were glistening glass and polished silver and damask naperies of snowlike whiteness. Covers had been removed from hot dishes containing lamb cutlets daintily trimmed and grilled and seasoned, the tenderest of fresh green peas, and other vegetables. Sweets that only a chef of genius could have devised, and hothouse fruits just picked from the royal conservatories with that virgin blue bloom upon them that rude fingers had not rubbed or spotted. There was nothing unusual or extravagant about this table. It was simply a thing well done.

In spite of the state of my nerves, I sat down to enjoy the sweet savour of the King's food, and lingered long over the luscious fruits and pale golden wine. The King at this hour must be lunching, I thought, so I did not hurry. The room I was in was evidently used as a sort of studio, a place devoted to these casual and hasty sittings. There was a large model stand or throne with a chair on it, several easels, and an absence of furniture, so that moving about was not interfered with. While I was wondering who had been the last to give sittings, and to what artist, the King's valet came in and asked what dress or uniform I would require, and if I expected the King to change. I said an Admiral's dress-coat and hat would do, and that I would only ask the King to wear the hat. He went away and returned with a coat, a hat and a form; on the latter he buttoned up the coat, arranged its fold and decorations, admonishing me to be particular about the stars and their places on the coat, because the Royal Family were very punctilious about this most important matter. He told me how often artists made mistakes in the details of dress, and pointed several out to me in large portraits hanging on the walls. He had charge of the King's Wardrobe, and had made a study of the appropriate dress or uniform for each occasion or function. After he had left me, the tall footmen came to take away the trays. After another interval some one came to say the King was arriving. The prolonged waiting had begun to affect my nerves, and it was now with a certain tremulousness that I watched the great door.

I began to wonder exactly how His Majesty would come, whether alone or accompanied, when the two doors opened very quietly, a small middle-aged man in a simple black dress stood in the middle of the doorway and said in a quiet tone, "The King." Stepping to one side with a slight inclination of his body to allow a still smaller man, in a plain blue serge suit to pass, I was confronted with the King, who, advancing briskly towards me, with a slight smile and outstretched hand, asked what he could do for me. As he took my hand I said, "Please, your Majesty, to put on that admiral's hat, and stand upon the throne in any easy position." Stepping up on the throne, he took the hat from the chair, and slapping it on his head in rather a jaunty manner, he said, "May I smoke?" Without waiting for my reply he took out a cigarette case, struck a match, lighted a good large cigarette, and smoked.

I had forgotten the clock. With a start I noted the hour, and with my usual and fatal conscientiousness, kept looking at it at short intervals in order not to allow the minute hand to overrun the twenty-minute mark by a hair's breadth, I was sketching nervously and timidly, the King was talking and puffing at his cigarette, and the clock was ticking. I was asked all about the sketch, what it was for, who had ordered it, and if I had begun it from a photograph before coming to the Palace. "You see," he said, "I have so little time to give to each of the many sittings required of me, that the artists paint in a head from a photograph at home first, and bring it here in a proper state to work on from me. That gives them a chance of doing something." He seemed surprised that I had not brought an unfinished drawing. The minute hand of the clock had fallen over two minute marks, as they sometimes do on their downward course from three to four, and it was fast approaching four, which was the limit of the twenty minutes. We talked on, but the next time I looked at the clock I became confused, for the hour and the minute hand had merged into one, and after that I could not tell one from the other. This was all to my advantage, because the hour hand remained a little after three, while the minute hand went marching on. But the confusion of mind sadly interfered with my work, and presently, when the minute hand did clearly stand upon four, and I knew that the time was up, I rose in despair and said, "The twenty minutes are gone." "Oh!" said the King, "that does not matter. You may go on if you wish." Plumping myself down again on the stool, I began to draw, and inwardly to bless Sir William Carrington and the clock, and time itself, for having robbed me of my independence and my self-reliance. The King chatted on until I found the drawing could not be redeemed because of the bad beginning, and then I rose again. At this His Majesty came quietly to me, glanced at it, and began to talk about lithography. He was interested in hearing that any paper could be used, as well as that prepared by a sort of size, and forgot all about the time, for he continued to listen and to talk for another half-hour, taking me at last around the galleries and corridors where the portraits are hung, and calling my attention to this one by Angèle and that one by Winterhalter. At last we came to that delightful study of his father, King Edward VII, by Bastien-Lepage, and there I lingered to wonder at its great charm, its technique and colour, and mentally to contrast that art with the coarse and vulgar work of the modern school.

The King was positive in his views upon painting, and freely expressed them. He wondered if he would ever get a satisfactory portrait of himself, that Cope had done the best portrait of his father, but that nearly all portraits were unsatisfactory in one way or another. The conversation between us was easy and unrestrained, and the King seemed to be in no hurry to break it off. In the room where he posed there were several full-length portraits, among them one of the Tsar of Russia, the ill-fated Nicholas. In this portrait the stars and decorations on the breast were irregularly placed and out of their true order, and this His Majesty pointed out to me, with the comment that painters were very careless about these matters, which were as important as precedence in ceremonial.

The man was speaking about things that belonged to the ritual of the throne as though the monarch in him were a thing apart, another ego. For he was to me at that moment the man only, the man who had paced the quarter-deck, the sportsman who walked the turnips and cut out clean rights and lefts from the coveys of little brown birds, or stopped rocketing pheasants in a gale of wind. He could throw off kinghood with the robes of the Star and Garter, and assume simple manhood with a blue serge coat and a billycock hat.

And yet withal that spiritual presence of the monarch made itself felt, for without a vestige, that was apparent, of the bearing, the tone of voice, or the other conventional things that one usually associates with princes, and of which some cannot divest themselves, the august presence of the chief among princes impressed one with a sense of awe.

True kingship is a spiritual thing. From the time of the rule of the Priest-Kings to Julius Cæsar, with the civil sceptre in one hand, and the pontifical sacrificing knife in the other, the spiritual nature of the chief of the state was married to the civil nature, and in modern times the little father of all the Russians was not only the head of the Church but also the chief magistrate, with universal jurisdiction over the civil courts. The divorcement of the civil from the religious power has left some trace of each in the other, and will do, so long as parenthood, with its obligations, its joys, and its sorrows, continues to be the basis of human institutions.

The institution of monarchy is pivotal. The nation may loyally revolve around its centre in a cohesive mass—the attraction to the centre following the analogy of the creative force of nature, while other systems are for the most part centrifugal, the chief symptom of which is disintegration. Lord Halsbury considered an autocratic government to be the best of all governments if the autocrat be a good man. From this primitive and essentially spiritual system the best derivative appears to be a constitutional monarchy.

THE KING'S HORSES

DEAN SWIFT, in that philosophic treatise called Gulliver's Travels, ostensibly written to amuse children, but in reality to ridicule the foibles of men, has placed the horse above men, or Yahoos, as he facetiously called them. I cannot do wrong, then, by including, with the men I have painted, some studies and observations I have made of those noble and distinguished creatures that live in the Royal Mews, behind Buckingham Palace, and known popularly as the "creams," or the State ponies.

Among the old titles of nobility in Russia is knias, a word that derives from kongne, a horse, and this title, knias, was given to the brothers of the king. Châteaubriand has said that all nobility comes from the horse. If the tradition of words is worth anything at all, and there is little doubt that words do give a truer insight into the past than most historians think, we have to conclude that Châteaubriand is right. Without pursuing the matter farther back than the French language, we find that the horse has always been associated with warriors, and from this warrior caste, and this only, nobility has been derived—the term chivalrous (chevalresque) meaning all that is elevated and refined in conduct. And it is a no less striking commentary upon the estimation given to the aristocratic horse that the followers of that King of England who was unfortunate because of his virtues rather than his vices—Charles I—were called "cavaliers," in distinction to the opposite and plebeian party, who were designated by the coarse and contemptuous name of "roundheads." That is, Swift would have described the followers of Cromwell and Milton—that rebellious poet who imagined a revolution in heaven—Yahoos, while the long-haired cavaliers would have been more to the refined taste of Gulliver, who, after a long sojourn as the guest of the Houyhnhnms in the odour of clover and sweet hay, on his return home was unable to bear the presence of his wife and

children because they smelt so abominably.
And as long hair, arranged in curls, was also at some periods affected by the noble cavaliers, so likewise the pure-bred Arabs are never docked and hogged, but wear their tails and manes long and flowing. This fashion is also a mark of the high office of the King's "creams," for as their service is to draw His Majesty's coach on state occasions, their manes and tails are dressed as carefully as a woman's hair; and when the gorgeous trappings are put on their backs, the most elaborate silken cords are woven in and out of the manes as adornments that add colour and lustre to the august processions of coronation days.
The following extracts from letters written at the time these studies were being made at the Royal Mews will describe more accurately than I can from memory the King's horses:—

Hotel Great Central, London.
November 9, 1911.

I was very well received by Captain Nicholas at the Royal Stables at Buckingham Palace. He has put the state coach and the cream-coloured horses at my service, giving me, in fact, the freedom of the stables and the coach house. He was good enough to indicate particularly "Pistachio" and "Vanilla" as fine animals. The latter has a coat like floss silk. The stables are very large and roomy and warm, so that I shall be exceedingly comfortable, and expect to enjoy myself immensely among the horses and the grooms.

* * * * *

Tuesday.

To-day has been beautiful and bright, but the sudden change to cold has shrivelled up all the people.
I had a long day over at the stables yesterday, and worked there again this morning. The horses look very well in the courtyard when the sun shines on them.

* * * * *

CROWN PRINCE

Buckingham Palace Hotel, London, S.W.
Thursday, 4.30 p.m.

A dark day! Four sketches of the horses are the result of the day's work. It seems droll enough that I should be drawing horses! They turned on the electric light so that I could continue after dark, and that enabled me to get in an outline or two. This morning I finished a drawing of "Crown Prince," who will be decked out in gay harness for me next Monday. I am inclined to come home to-morrow evening in the five o'clock train, and leave early on Monday morning so as to reach the Mews at one o'clock. There is nothing new to tell you: everything was very quiet and peaceful in the stables. There are eleven creams in all, and more at Hampton Court, where they are bred.

* * * * *

November 15, 1911.

Another day is nearly gone, and there are two sketches—a view of the side of the coach, and a more elaborated study than usual of "Vanilla." This horse has a coat like floss silk: another has wavy hair on its legs which resembles without colour the markings on a zebra. To-day was visitors' day, and I had to stop work at half-past two. I did the coach first, and when the stables were in order worked on the horse. The grooms are very attentive, and look after me well. One stands by to keep the horse in order. Captain Nicholas came through the stables to-day, greeting me cheerily as he passed with some foreign person. He said he would take care of me. The old porter at the entrance to the Mews is the father-in-law of the head groom, Slack. The two men are very genial characters. It seems that many years ago Queen Victoria presented a History of the Painters of England to the porter, and he gave it to his son-in-law, who faithfully read it. He knows all about Reynolds and Gainsborough, and goes frequently to the National Gallery to see the masterpieces. This will amuse Clara. To-morrow I shall work in the courtyard, where the creams are to be exercised, from 10 to 11.30; after that the harness will be put on "Crown Prince" for me.
What an amusing paper is the Daily Sketch, that Clara has sent me! How jubilant they all are! I dread Balfour's exit rather than Law's entrance. What a good omen his name bears! George R. Sims is bound to use it as dressing to his "Mustard and Cress."

* * * * *

November 15, 1911.

The days go by very quickly while I am at work, but the evenings are long. When the work is done, and I leave the gateway of the stables, I suddenly bethink me, with a rather unpleasant mingling of surprise and depression, that I am not going home, but to the hotel.

It is not a very large hotel. It seems to be filled with old-fashioned families from the country; but I am not sure—they may be Londoners, out of servants.

The Royal Stables are spacious, one on each side of the great courtyard. To the right are installed the eight creams and eight blacks, on the left are the carriage horses, fine tall bays. To-day was visitors' day, and before I left a great many people were strolling in.

The sires of these horses were given to the young Queen Victoria by the King of Hanover. They are stout, dimpled creatures, with pink faces and pale eyes. The coach was used at the coronation of King George III, about 1760. There should be a history of the horses in the offices of the stables, and I shall ask Captain Nicholas for it when I see him again.

It is a great business, this stable-keeping, for the King. An army of men look after the horses and coaches, and the place must be filled with their families. I hear the voices of children everywhere.

* * * * *

Friday.

Yesterday I had almost decided to return to Warwick this evening, but to-day was clear, until late in the afternoon, and I worked on in the stables until nearly five o'clock.

The result of the four days' work is ten pastel drawings and one sketch in oil. The horses grow to be more beautiful every day. They are queer creatures, just like some old Chinese emperor who never shows himself to the world. They live a secluded and exclusive life, so that the public may be awed into wonderment when they appear with all their gorgeous trappings on. I believe they are the only aristocrats left in England! And they have such ugly red-pink noses and small, pale eyes!

The grooms are all very ordinary-looking men, mostly young, but the head groom is a man of forty—very small and very capable.

The horses are docile and mannerly. They are trained first at Hampton Court, and afterwards in London. There are eleven here, and I do not know how many at Hampton Court.

Next Monday the gala harness is to be put on "Crown Prince." It is a great undertaking, for his mane has to be plaited. When the harness is on, very little of the horse can be seen.

* * * * *

November 20, 1911.

When I entered the stables this morning there were four men at work dressing "Crown Prince" and putting the last touches on his toilet. Slack, the head groom, was perched up on a high bench, so that he could reach the mane of the gorgeously bedecked aristocrat. The horse seemed to be smothered in red and gold and purple, and, in the subdued light of the stable, looked more magnificent than he does in the street, when he is drawing the state coach.

I started work at once, and did not stop an instant until after half-past five. The result is four sketches—a large head, a front view, a back view, and the study in oils. The horse was fretting and fuming at the finish, but I was sorry I could not go on all night. You have no idea of the beauty of the great creature in his trappings.

They allowed me to watch the disrobing. The purple rosettes were taken from the mane, and the mane was taken out of plait, and slowly and carefully all the heavy harness was taken off. When the bridle was pulled from him his face gleamed out pale and pink, with two small, angry eyes shining in the glimmer of the electric light hanging just over him.

* * * * *

November 22, 1911.

I have just come in from the stables, where I made three more sketches, this time of the horses' heads, which are more difficult than their tails. It seems almost presumptuous in me to attempt, without any former and prolonged experience in the drawing of animals, this kind of work; and to begin on the bodies of those precious aristocrats, the "cream" of society among horses, the exclusive eight, as it were, is like putting sacrilegious and unblessed hands upon things that are holy. The fool gets more out of life than the angel, I shrewdly suspect, and always when there is some "wit" closely allied to his fooling.

The noble "Pistachio" has been holding a levée, and while his royal nose was being wiped, his mane brushed and combed, and his sleek and glossy coat rubbed down by the deft and diminutive Slack, his portrait was painted, in the presence of a small company of gentlemen-in-waiting, or grooms of the chamber. The unusual experience created a biting appetite towards the end of the sitting, for he began to yawn, to whinny, and at last to neigh imperatively for his oats, which, after much teasing by the sieve-bearer, were given him.

Three sketches were made in two hours. I really should have made more.

* * * * *

November 23, 1911.

The horses were out exercising this morning, but the wind was so strong and cold that I dared not stand to work. After watching them march and manoeuvre for ten or fifteen minutes, I retreated into the warm stables and chatted with the manager, or whatever his official designation may be. He has promised to rig out a groom, or postilion, in his state dress, so that I may make a study of him as he appears on coronation days and the opening of Parliament.

I went to the Scala last evening and stayed until the coronation procession was put on the screen. After all, the horses appear but twice, and for a few seconds only. The second time is when the sword is presented to the King, and the royal carriage then takes up the whole of the picture, and the horses are blotted out. The manager of the theatre told me I might find almost anything at 82, Wardour Street, so I am going there to look over the films and pictures.

Yesterday a young porter at the gates told me he had taken pictures of the state coach, and I bought two. They are very sharp indeed, and show every detail. Next month, when the coach is taken out to wash, I shall get him to take a picture of it in the position I require. He will also take the horses for me as they are exercised in the luggage van.

*****

February 14, 1912.

The day at the stables has been one of the most interesting I have ever known. The horses were quietly magnificent, and the processes of harnessing and dressing exceedingly entertaining and instructive. After the return from the opening of Parliament, there was a little more hurry and a little less form in getting rid of the gold lace; but even that made a picture in the stables, in the dull afternoon light, that I shall remember for long. It has been a full day, and I hope to be able to make good use of what I saw.

MR GLADSTONE

I.—AT HAWARDEN CASTLE

SHORTLY after I had settled in Alpha House three of the many beautiful daughters of Mr. Joseph Rowley, "Taffy" in Du Maurier's "Trilby," came to see me. While having tea in the garden under the shade of the great weeping ash-tree which was said by the Princess Dolgorouki, who lived there as a girl, to be the largest in England, I could not help noticing the resemblance of the three sisters to Romney's portraits of Lady Hamilton, and particularly to Ethel, Mrs. Myles Kennedy, whose commanding beauty, as I afterwards was to discover, arrested attention wherever she appeared. The conversation naturally turned upon Romney, the portraits, and Emma Lyon herself, who, as a young girl, lived in the parish of Hawarden, near the Gladstones, the Glynnes and the Rowleys, in whose families traces of a similar and remarkable beauty could be found: the Romney portrait of Lady Hamilton in the gallery of Tabley Hall, Cheshire, was always called "Mrs. Gladstone," from the striking resemblance. The outcome of the talk was a suggestion from Maud, who afterwards became Mrs. Strickland, that I ought to paint Mr. Gladstone, and Alice agreed to take me to Hawarden Castle and introduce me to Mrs. Gladstone and Mrs. Drew, if I would care to spend a month on the banks of the Dee.

Here was an opportunity that could not be lightly put aside. My regular work had been interrupted by several years of travel in Italy and in America, and having once more settled down in London, as I thought, permanently, in a comfortable house, surrounded by a garden of unusual size and beauty, I saw, in this proposal to paint the foremost statesman in Europe, the beginning of a prosperous and interesting career. After a little discussion and some subsequent correspondence, these young ladies engaged rooms in the inn at Queen's Ferry, where the most momentous month of my life, in some respects, was passed. The morning after our arrival we visited "Taffy" and Mrs. Rowley at Dee Bank, and were introduced to the other daughters. There I was interested to find a complete set of Whistler's first etchings, subscribed for in Paris by "Taffy" when the master was entering upon that turbulent and eventful life-struggle that bore him—but alas! only after his death—to the most exalted position among the few men of genius in Art.

The ladies drove me, as they had promised, to Hawarden Castle and introduced me to Mr. and Mrs. Gladstone and Mrs. Drew. Mr. Gladstone received me affably, and listened with great good nature to my request for a sitting. It was immediately arranged that I should make a drawing next day. It is needless to describe the amount of gladness that filled me to overflowing as we drove merrily back to Dee Bank, and subsequently to the inn, to impart the good news to delighted audiences.

The next morning I prepared my papers and pastels and started to walk to the castle. There are times when the mind dominates the body so completely as practically to annihilate it. The senses respond to impressions from without and from within which seem to be transmitted to the brain by spiritual rather than corporeal processes. At such moments forgetful enthusiasts are misled into thinking that the body and the spirit are divisible and can exist independently of each other. The air caresses you as you move over rough stones without feeling them: the heavens bathe your vision in a flood of azure, and the song of the lark thrills you without passing through your ears: the scent of hedgerows and of honeysuckle embalms you completely and makes you one with the ambient air.

Such was my condition of being as I quickly traversed the distance between the ferry and the lower entrance to the churchyard which I crossed to shorten the walk to the castle gates. Here it was that I regained consciousness, with a very large dose of self-consciousness thrown in. I began to lose my way, and, instead of taking the narrow path through a small wooden gate, I continued on the drive that leads across the park, and a great discouragement fell upon me. "What if I should fail?" became an oft-repeated question to myself; and so questioning I stumbled up a grassy slope towards the wall into which was built a narrow door. When I was near enough to see them, three letters and a date on the lintel became distinct. The word I read was W. E. G., and the date, 1853, was the year of my birth. The word translated into English meant "way," but standing under the lintel the period after each capital letter indicated them to be the initials of a name. Slowly I began to say "William Ewart Gladstone," and with a lighter heart I laughed aloud, and, lifting the latch, entered into the grounds and gardens of the castle.

That morning I made two pastel drawings of Mr. Gladstone, one reading and the other writing. They seemed to be so satisfactory to Mrs. Gladstone and Mrs. Drew, that I was encouraged to ask for sittings for a portrait, and it was then and there agreed between Mr. Gladstone and myself that I could come to the "Temple of Peace" in the mornings and paint, if I did not ask for formal sittings. In other words, Mr. Gladstone would spend his time in reading and writing, according to his daily routine, and I could catch him as I found him. He was to do his work and I mine, without considering one the other. That arrangement suited me perfectly. Here was a new aspect of portraiture, and one that strongly appealed to the passive side of my indolent nature. Why should I not take advantage of this unforeseen permission to paint portraits at my ease, and so be free from the ever-trammelling thought that my sitter was being victimized through being obliged to stare stolidly at the antics and flourishes of an uninspired and uninspiring painter? Are there not enough stark and stiff upright figures looking down at us from the walls of every public and private gallery in the universe, that I should add one more senseless effigy to the number, unless commissioned to do so by a wife who avers that her husband is always upright and his eyes brilliant? From that day to this I have set my face steadily against the formal staring portrait, and, whenever it has been possible, have painted men at home, and in their homes, always avoiding anything like studio lights and effects.

The day after this interview I began that series of paintings of Mr. Gladstone that show him in his hours of peaceful recreation and leisure at Hawarden, and in his intervals of rest in Downing Street. The next day I began the first of the series on a canvas measuring 24 X 18. The day after, the colours in the head were evenly

MR. GLADSTONE
At Downing Street

sticky and in a state of drying. At the end of the sitting there appeared upon the canvas the head of a wrinkled old man that bore no resemblance to Mr. Gladstone. Yet it was finished: there was nothing more to be done to it. It reminded me of those minutely executed Italian paintings of old men carrying bottles of chianti wine. Its surface was shiny and its technique offensive to the eye. When I removed the protecting canvas on reaching the inn and looked at it there, and showed it to my wife, we both sadly admitted that it was a failure, an irredeemable failure.

In the early morning, on looking again at the head, it seemed to have degenerated still more by drying hard. Turning it to the wall, I breakfasted without appetite, and drove away with another canvas to try again. This time I selected Mr. Gladstone's writing attitude, and painted in a different style, using very little colour and no medium. The colours I used were ground in petroleum, and petroleum was my medium, when I used any.

How the previous head had become so shiny puzzled me. Having been more successful with the writing portrait, I returned home in better spirits. Looking again at the first head, I suddenly remembered that cuttle-fish bone would rub down the surface of the paint and remove the objectionable gloss. The canvas on which it was painted was French twill and woven evenly, so I did not fear the removal of the paint in spots or blotches. Taking a little water and sprinkling it over the painting, I began to rub gently with the cuttle-fish, after having removed its hard and bony edges. Presently a semi-transparent film composed of particles of cuttle-fish and of paint, held in the water, covered the head like a veil. To my surprise and joy the colour as well as the texture of the face changed completely, and with the change in colour there appeared a decided likeness to Mr. Gladstone. I called my wife, who instantly recognized the change, and exclaimed, "Why, you can make it like with very little." Having sufficiently rubbed off the surface, I dried the canvas, and cleaned it with petroleum. Then taking the palette I made a colour similar to the film I had removed, and scumbled over the head with it, so that the work and detail all appeared through it. This was a good surface to work into while still wet, so I hurried off to the castle, where I found Mr. Gladstone reading, and in the same light and position as in the portrait.

As I worked, putting in an accent here and a light there, and enhancing the reflected light from the book on the face, the resemblance so much strengthened that it brought forth an exclamation of pleasure from Mrs. Drew when she entered the room, as she was in the habit of doing, to see how I was progressing. I began to feel that this small portrait was really growing under my brush, and had risen to a happy frame of mind, when an untoward and strange thing happened. There was a visitor at the castle, Lady Phillimore. I had met her at tea in the drawing-room the day before. She suddenly appeared behind me and asked me in a whisper to join her in the drawing-room, as she had something to say to me. Imagine my feelings! I knew that Mr. Gladstone would stop reading in a few minutes. I could not ask him to continue, as we had agreed upon perfect liberty of action. The portrait could not be painted on the following day, because the paint would be dry, and dry paint cannot be worked into. It can be worked upon only, and that spoils it. A few minutes more would finish the head, and I was asked to give those precious minutes to this lady!

With my usual complaisance I sacrificed my work and went to her in the drawing-room. "Mr. Hamilton," she began, "I only wanted to expostulate with you for wasting Mr. Gladstone's time, and yours for that matter. Don't you know that Sir John Millais has painted Mr. Gladstone, and that is enough? You cannot expect to succeed where so many other men have failed. Mr. Gladstone is a very busy man, and he should not be disturbed in his work." "But, Madam," I protested, "we have arranged all that." "No, no, it must worry him;" and she continued on in this strain until I began to feel that this lady might possibly be the mouthpiece of a member of the family, and that it would be well to take her counsel and give up the sitting. I acquiesced and returned to the library, where I found Mr. Gladstone still reading. "At any cost," I thought, "I will work until he moves," and hurriedly began to paint. In a moment or two another lady came to me and said quietly, "Go on with your work, and don't mind mama. She is over-zealous." The portrait was finished there and then. I have never known whether Mr. Gladstone had not been a silent witness to these proceedings, and in consequence prolonged his reading for the purpose of aiding me. His thoughtfulness on subsequent occasions more than leads me to believe that he was always conscious of what transpired about him without in the least appearing to be. The hour spent that morning in finishing this portrait was probably the most intensely interesting episode of all my experience in portrait painting. The circumstances all combined to create a tumult of ideas that inspired and invigorated me. The man I was painting, what he stood for in the Empire, his picturesqueness, his surroundings, the contrast of great power and extreme simplicity, and above all, to me, the ease and comfort of working before one who seemed to be absolutely unconscious of my presence. Had it not been for the momentary intrusion of an officious and self-appointed bodyguard, my contentment would have been complete. How many geniuses have had these body-guards, some permanent, some transitory! Johnson had his Boswell, Swinburne his Watts-Dunton, Ruskin his Severn, Whistler his Pennell.

I protected the little head with great care so that it should not be rubbed on its way to the inn. Taking my seat in the dog-cart that was waiting for me, I drove rapidly down the hill into the fields below, where ripening corn was waving in golden billows against the distant blue of the estuary of the Dee. My eyes saw what Tennyson made "The Lady of Shalott" see—

Long fields of barley and of rye,
That clothe the wold and meet the sky—

and I was filled with a vision of plenty and of gladness. The visit to Queen's Ferry had not been in vain. Memories of those happy days still linger but little dimmed by the more than thirty years that intervene between then and now, crowded as they have been by ever-changing acts and scenes of a long and full life.

II.—THE STORY OF THE PROPHETIC BUTTERFLY

THE rôle that the butterfly plays in nature had remained entirely unambiguous until that paradoxical genius, James McNeill Whistler, found in its innocent, gaudy, and harmless image a symbol to emphasize the malignant enmity of his enemies. When he descanted on the

MR. GLADSTONE
(By J. McLure Hamilton)

persecution by the critics, which followed his slight, airy, and fantastic imaginations, nocturnes in blue and gold, he aptly described the process as "crushing a butterfly on the wheel." Here then was the giddy and insouciant creature of the scent-laden ether drawn down to suffer one of the heaviest and cruellest punishments devised by the ingenuity of those other creatures who are said to be a little lower than the angels. The happy allusion gave the great master his monogram, but he added a sting to the tail—another of his facetious ways of saying that "nature is looking up."

The butterfly you are to hear about is of another sort, one of those fluttering pale things, like the petals of an evening primrose, that joyously disport themselves among the chestnut-trees of the Champs Élysées, in that atmosphere only found in Paris when Spring has dressed the gay city in tones of tender green under the genial skies of May. Onslow Ford and I, with other painters and sculptors, were in the habit of making annual pilgrimages to Paris to see the Salon. In those days the exhibition was held in the Palais de l'Industrie; the new Salon, of the secessionists—for there must be revolutionaries in Art as well as in religion and politics—was housed in the building at the Champs de Mars.

As Ford and I were walking up the right side of the avenue in the direction of the Arc de Triomphe, he called my attention to the coveys of primrose-yellow butterflies, and said, "Whenever one of these floats down and alights on my coat or hat, it is an omen of good fortune, not to me, but to the man who happens to be walking with me. If one should alight on me now, you will get a medal or something," adding rather sadly, "I never get anything." He had hardly finished speaking when one of the graceful insects settled composedly on the lapel of his coat, and began that quaint custom of the butterfly of slowly opening and shutting its wings. The little portrait of Gladstone was in the exhibition. My feelings were aroused, in spite of the flash of cold reason that I bring to bear upon all things called superstitious, and, as I listened to Ford's tale of awards that always followed the visit of the prophetic butterfly, my eagerness to see the fulfilment of the prophecy made me quicken my steps towards the entrance of the great building close at hand. So unlike the raven perched upon the marble bust of Pallas, croaking "never more," was this other winged thing, luminous as that wonderful crescent distinct with a duplicate horn, lightly poised on the dark coat of Onslow Ford, that I almost began to believe the potency of the message, and that its tidings might be of joyful import.

We entered the great hall of sculpture, and here the papillon took flight and volleyed about in graceful curves among the bronzes and marbles and plaster casts that encumbered without embellishing the lofty conservatory. Ford's attention was diverted at once to the sculpture; the last Dallou, the Fremiet, or the Rodin must be seen, and his own work searched out among the myriads of exhibits.

At last we were in the picture galleries, and presently I espied the little portrait, and on the frame was a yellow placard. With an increased beating of the pulse I hurried to the picture, exclaiming, "'Mention Honorable!' Ford; you see the oracle spoke truly." I was satisfied. Had it been a medal, perhaps my pleasure would have been just a shade greater. I do not know. But this was not all; like the honours announced to Macbeth, the greater was to come. On returning to the hotel I found a formal communication from the Minister of the Fine Arts requesting me to sell the picture to the State! No wonder the little emissary of good fortune had lingered so long with us!

"Sell it by all means," Ford called out after I had read the letter; "never mind the price. I would give almost anything for this honour."

In those days it was a much-coveted distinction among English and American artists to be represented in the collection of Modern Art which the French Government was bringing together in the Luxembourg Museum. Before that year, if I am not mistaken, only one foreign picture hung in the gallery. That year Sargent's Carmencita, Whistler's Mother, and the little Gladstone were added. Whistler, so I am told, resented the inclusion of the small portrait in the same class as that of the Mother and, if the story is not exaggerated, exclaimed, "Why drag in Hamilton! Who is he, anyhow? "Alas for human foresight! He lived long enough to discover me as an "enemy."

There was great rejoicing in the cabarets that night, as, arm-in-arm, we wandered through the mazes of the Latin Quarter, seeking out the old haunts of my student days and ending again in the allées of the Champs Élysées scintillating with lamps of all shades of colour, where we listened to Aristide Bruant dans son café.

The episode was ended. A silver chain had been forged in Paris many years before by Svengali, the wizard. When "Taffy," that splendid type of British athlete, had linked his strong arm into the arms of Poynter and Whistler and Du Maurier, he began unwittingly a story that ended twenty years later under the same flowering trees of the Champs Élysées; a tale that was continued and deftly woven by the graceful hands of his then unborn daughters, who came, as the Three Graces, to lead the way through the groves of Hawarden back to the shrine where Art is the goddess adored by a universal brotherhood of worshippers.

III.—AT DOWNING STREET

MR. GLADSTONE was again Prime Minister. He was living at No. 10, Downing Street, that unpretentious old house whose walls echoed and re-echoed the mandates of the governors of the British Empire.

I sought anew the Prime Minister and asked to be allowed to work as I had worked before: America wanted a portrait. He consented with the simplicity of manner and grace which one expects from a great man. I was to come early in the morning after breakfast. "At ten o'clock Sir Algernon West, my secretary, will bring in the letters, and he and I will go over them together. It will take perhaps twenty minutes or less. In case there should be anything of a private nature to which you should not be privy, I will ask you to wait in the next room for the few minutes required to discuss the answer." After a pause, "But no," he continued, "on second thoughts I will go with Sir Algernon into this ante-room, so that you may go on with your work during the few minutes I shall be absent." I thanked him for his consideration, and sat down before the easel, knowing how very dear to those who can command is the virtue of acquiescence.

Mr. Gladstone then stretched himself out on a dark-red morocco sofa that was drawn up diagonally across one of the tall windows with its foot towards the door, and began to read. There was an ample space between the window and the sofa to accommodate a chair placed immediately back of the sofa. I had worked for about an hour when the door at the foot of the sofa opened and a tall, well-dressed man entered, bearing in his hand a large bundle of papers opened flat. After saying "Good morning" and glancing at me with a little surprise in his eyebrows, he sat down in the chair behind the sofa and, drawing it forward, faced Mr. Gladstone, who dropped his book and looked at him in an attitude of attention. Sir Algernon West began without preamble to read the letters and other communications, to which Mr. Gladstone gave his replies—"Yes" or "No"—without comment, or in a few words indicated the general tenor of the reply, leaving it to the well-trained mind of Sir Algernon to amplify. Now and again Mr. Gladstone would interrupt the reading of a long letter, or of any very important or perhaps personal appeal, and taking it, would say, "I will answer that myself."

It is impossible for me now to recall what Sir Algernon West said in regard to letters of a private character intended only for Mr. Gladstone's information, but I do remember that he told Sir Algernon he had arranged to have them read in the adjoining room. On one or two occasions the Prime Minister and his secretary left me for a few minutes, but this happened, I was glad to note, very rarely, as it occasioned me not a little embarrassment to think that my presence caused the Prime Minister the inconvenience of rising from his resting position on the couch. Mr. Gladstone knew the art of resting. His strength and activity were unusual in men of his age, but he wasted neither, so that he could call at once upon all his reserves and use them in any emergency. So soon as the secretary left the room, Mr. Gladstone would rise with the letters he had retained and go to his desk and begin to write the answers slowly and carefully in that well-known small handwriting that indicates the literary or careful and methodic mind. We worked in silence. Big Ben chimed the hours. The faces of statesmen looked down from the walls upon a scene that must have recalled many a similar episode in their own lives, for the drawings, mostly by Richmond the elder, were in themselves evidence of the relation between portrait-painter and patron.

Mr. Gladstone was, to me, very beautiful. I never tired of admiring him, and was always filled with the desire to paint or draw him in every pose he assumed. His colour was luminous; that is, his face seemed to irradiate light, to reflect light where most faces absorb it. These luminous faces are rare in women and more so in men. My niece, Norah, to whom I wrote the letter describing Bismarck, had the most luminous complexion in face and hair of anyone I have seen. This luminosity has been sought for by painters, of landscape chiefly, and Monet discovered that by leaving projecting particles of paint in a precise rather than an irregular pattern all over the surface of the canvas he was able to procure a greater impression of "open air" than by the ordinary manipulation of the paint. The explanation is simple. Each projecting point of paint caught a ray of light and projected a shadow, and the general effect became in consequence more brilliant. When age and cleaning has rubbed these points away the picture will assume a general dullness.

People whose faces have been pitted in small, almost invisible and regular, pits by small-pox seem to throw off light. Each pit is a concave reflector, and its lower half catches the light from above and reflects it as from a cup. The face of Mr. Gladstone when last in Downing Street was covered with regular and small wrinkles that were only visible in certain lights. These small lines may have caused in him the effect I have been trying to explain.

While bending over the writing-table the reflected light from the white paper produced an effect, in combination with his thin white and rather straggling hair, that always inspired the most irresistible desire to sketch quickly each succeeding phase.

Work went on, in this regular routine, day after day until the portrait, a full-length but under life-size, was almost finished. But one morning Mrs. Gladstone came into the room, and she in turn seemed surprised to see me calmly working while Sir Algernon West was going over the correspondence. I rose to greet her, but she nodded and passed by me on her way to the window, where for a few moments she stood gazing out towards the Duke of York's Column. Presently she came back and, leaning over me, said, "I do not think you should be here while Sir Algernon is reading the letters: there may be things in them that you should not know."

"Yes," I replied, "that is so, but Mr. Gladstone has arranged all that. I am to go out, or Mr. Gladstone will take Sir Algernon into the next room when anything I should not hear comes up." Slowly and reluctantly she appeared to accept this, but after another and longer inspection of St. James's Park from the window she began to pass nervously to and fro between Mr. Gladstone and me. Presently Mr. Gladstone raised his voice a little above the tone he was using with the secretary, and I heard him say, "My dear! do not walk between Mr. Hamilton and me. You will prevent him from seeing me." I almost shuddered to think of the effect of this admonition upon Mrs. Gladstone, for there seemed to be in the manner and the tone a slight rebuke. I was not wrong, for after another but shorter view out of the window, Mrs. Gladstone returned to the easel, and looking over it so that Mr. Gladstone could not see her face, she said firmly and decisively, "Mr. Hamilton, I know you should not be here. It must be an embarrassment to Sir Algernon to have you in the room when he is here." That finished the matter and, rising, I said, "Very well, Mrs. Gladstone, I will go out until the letters are finished." As I moved away Mr. Gladstone turned his head towards me, and I still remember the faintest of smiles and the most innocent of winks to console me for the disturbance. There is no doubt that, technically speaking, Mrs. Gladstone was right, although there had been nothing in the correspondence that could not have been shouted from the housetops, and I was so little curious, and my work so absorbing, that most of it made no impression upon me, yet in an unguarded moment something unusual might have been read that my ears should not have heard.

This was the second time that work on a portrait had been interrupted by a mischance, and, as I shall show in the next article, which deals with the making of a third and the last portrait, an interruption of a different kind almost prevented its completion.

About two years after the foregoing incident, while on a shooting expedition with a score or more of wild young spirits in the Matilija Canyon of the Sierra Nevadas, east of Santa Barbara, in Lower California, a telephone message came to me in those lonely and distant mountains that Mr. Edward H. Coates, the president of the Pennsylvania Academy of the Fine Arts, had acquired this portrait. No

MR. GLADSTONE
In the Temple of Peace

contrast could have been greater than that between the cabaret of Aristide Bruant among the lights of the Champs Élysées and the lonely ranch house, on the then barren shores of Lake Guadalupe, but the rejoicing was the same, although enlivened by whisky-floats instead of vin rouge.

IV.—IN THE TEMPLE OF PEACE

I AM once more at Hawarden. In the Temple of Peace there is absolute silence. An older Gladstone is sitting at the desk by the tall window that overlooks the green slope that rises to the hill on which the ruins of the ancient castle stand: a little shrunken maybe—not quite so vigorous—but more beautiful than ever. He writes with his head bent down close to the paper on the table, and every now and then refers to a blue-bound book lying at hand.

The canvas on my easel is small, the same as the first that was painted in the library years before. He raises his head sometimes and gazes thoughtfully out upon the trees that are changing the colour of their leaves to yellow, pink, and chestnut. The profile against the pane is so finely cut that I trace its outline in the lower corner of the canvas, and go on with the portrait when he bends his head to write. Mr. Gladstone is editing the works of Bishop Butler. Presently, wishing to make a comprehensive search through the pages of the blue volume, he takes it up in one hand, and using the thumb as a ratchet, allows the leaves to fall one by one, seeking on each page the thought or phrase to suit his purpose. I pause in my work and wait until he resumes his position writing, but the minutes go slowly by, and still the leaves fall one by one until the whole attitude and expression begin to appeal to me as something to paint, and to paint at once. But will he hold the book in that queer way long enough? Over against the wall on the other side of the room is a canvas, but larger than I need. In an instant it is on the easel and I have measured by the eye the spot on which to place the head. With the greatest rapidity of which I am capable I brushed in the colour, the thin gray hair, the shadowed but luminous face, the eye-sockets, and a few lines for the pursed lips. Every nerve was awake and strained to speed on the eye and hand before the book was dropped, never to be taken up again in the same way. It seemed a miracle that it was held so long—how long I have never been able to tell, but, judging by the work done, full twenty minutes must have slipped slowly away before the hand began to droop and the blue volume fell upon the table—and my heart fell with it. There was a daub of colour on the canvas and nothing more. Sad and disappointed, I carried it back to its place against the wall, muttering, "Another good canvas spoiled," and resumed the portrait writing. This I finished. (Lord Armitstead saw it at Agnew's some time afterwards, and gave it to Lord Gladstone. The profile remains in the corner.) As I was about to start work I noticed that Mr. Gladstone commenced to nod the head a little, and was inclined to sleep. Rising suddenly, he left the desk and passed across the room to the other window, sat down comfortably in an easy chair and went to sleep. "This is the end of work to-day," I thought, so I began to pack up my things. To do so I had to cross the floor in front of the sleeper, when, to my astonishment and delight, I found Mr. Gladstone's head was in the same position in relation to the light as in the sketch with the blue book which I had rubbed in. Seizing the canvas, it took me but a second to move the easel to a position near, and directly in front of, Mr. Gladstone's chair. By looking down upon him the view became perfect, and I commenced deliberately and carefully to put in the details. I knew that the slumber was profound, and that it would last for at least thirty minutes, and there was no danger of disturbing it with any noise that I might make, because of his deafness. So I was quite composed and happy, and worked away merrily. The eyes had been sufficiently indicated at first, so I confined my attention to the forms of the head and face, and to the mouth, which, mirabile dictu, was pursed up as it had been when reading the pages of the book. Before the nap was over the portrait was completed, and it was not touched again. There was the head on a tall, bare canvas, and the lines of a book, and a finger. Moving the easel back to its first position in front of the other window, it did not take long to sketch in the position of the desk with the papers on it, and to indicate the high window, and the lawn sloping upwards to the ancient ruin on the hill. The details of the background were added afterwards, the bookcase, I believe, in Edward Clifford's drawing-room in Kensington Square.

And so ended a long series of portraits and sketches of the most famous man of his century.

Mr. Gladstone was a tall and strong man; his massive head surpassed in character and in beauty that of all other men of his time. The mobility of his features and his comprehensive range of expression seconded, in the most extraordinary degree, a voice as resonant as a bell, clanging in command or appealing in rhythmic and silvery tones. No tragedian that I have seen, from the young American Booth to the English Irving, or among the Italians, headed by Salvini, had a tithe of his facial play. I have seen him turn suddenly from a ministering into an avenging angel. With his grandchild, Dorothy Drew, on one knee and the black pomeranian on the other, his countenance would light up, as though he were possessed of all the beatitudes. When speaking of the wrongs of nations or of peoples, his righteous frown might have bespoken the minister of divine vengeance.

I did not know the extent and variety of his more subtle expressions. Indeed, I am inclined to think that subtle emotions played but a small part in his large nature, the extremes of affection and of hatred being the dominating impulses of one who lived but in two spheres, a public and a private, the former for and with the people, the other in and for the family.

I happened to be in the House of Commons and was sitting in the small gallery just above the floor of the House when Mr. Gladstone rose to attack Mr. Chamberlain, after the Home Rule split. He was magnificent; his thin silvery hair was so lighted up that it looked like a great mass of white.

Thrusting his fingers through it with a majestic gesture, he began: "There is an office in the Church of Rome presided over by the Devil's Advocate whose duty it is to defend the Satanic Majesty from attack; and if there is a man in this House, aye, even in this country, qualified for the office, it is the Right Hon. Member for Birmingham. (Applause and laughter.)

The reason for supposing, as some have done, that Mr. Gladstone was a small man, is that he always sat on the Front Treasury or Opposition Bench beside or near Sir William Harcourt, whose bulk overarched every one else. There is in the word "massive" a meaning that goes deeper than mere mass. Mr. Gladstone's massiveness resembled chiselled granite. Sir William Harcourt was also massive, but that was mere flesh.

There was nothing more than that which is common to most sound and strong men in Bismarck's head, save two features, one of which was unnatural, and the other merely a decoration. His head was round and solid, his nose short and insignificant, his mouth and chin strong, his forehead full, but not high. The two chief features were not features at all, but abnormalities—for his eyes, round and full, projected unpleasantly from their sockets, and the hairs of his eyebrows stood out like quills on a fretful porcupine. Gladstone, on the other hand, without any abnormality in particular, was, in old age, whatever he may have been in youth, as a whole, super-normal. The forehead was not high, and sloped backwards from the frontal bones that overhung the eye-sockets, where dark and piercing eyes were deep set. The head was very broad and full at the temples, a marked characteristic of most politicians and statesmen—in Balfour the distance from the ears to the top of the head is unusually great, but the head is narrow—Gladstone's nose was large and masterful, the mouth firm, and the chin broad, and not prominent. But the style of the bone structure was quite different from that of other men, in that all the fine points which are usually thought to be associated with genius or talent were in him pronounced, rather than exaggerated.

The iris was fringed with a conspicuous arcus senilis. I have known but one other like it, and that in a comparatively young man.

His large brain must have been composed of memory cells which increased by use to supply a great and continually growing need. He was self-centred. No one can accuse him of ambition, because his life was not the fulfilment of his desires: all things seemed to come to him before he had time to desire them; in other words, success often anticipated desire.

BISMARCK

AMONG the visitors to London in the summer of the year when the butterfly fluttered to the shoulder of Onslow Ford, in the allée of the Champs Élysées—to presage the honour conferred by the French Government upon the small portrait of Gladstone—was Professor Anton von Werner of Berlin, the painter of the historical pictures illustrating the scenes of the great war of 1870, in which Bismarck figures so prominently.

Professor von Werner praised the "Gladstone," and said to me, "You should paint Bismarck. I will give you a letter to him, if you will come over to Berlin." This seemed naturally to follow out the idea I had imagined of doing portraits of great men; so I made ready for a visit to the Continent by letting Alpha House to Sarah Bernhardt, who was then commencing a series of representations at, I believe, the Lyceum Theatre.

Crossing to Boulogne, we passed a short distance up the coast to Wimereux, where Alfred Gilbert had taken a villa for the summer. Rooms were engaged in the hotel for Mrs. Hamilton, my mother, and George, and after a few days in their company by the sea, I started by the way of Brussels, Antwerp, and Amsterdam for Berlin.

The galleries in Belgium and Holland are the richest in fine specimens of the Old Masters of any in Europe. Among the collections is the group of paintings by Franz Hals, at Haarlem. In these portraits Hals shows himself to be the master painter. Every excelling quality, even that of rich and superb colour, rivalling, if not surpassing, the Venetians, can be found in this dozen or more canvases.

The journey from Amsterdam to Berlin was monotonous and fatiguing. The fields were well cultivated, but there were no farm-houses, as in Holland; the dwellings seemed to be clustered in small, scattered villages.

The account of my journey is more clearly set forth in the following letters, chiefly to my wife, than any narrative from recollection of events that happened so long ago could possibly describe:—

KISSINGEN.
Saturday Evening, July 17, 1892.

My dear Clara,
I have just had a note from Prince Bismarck's secretary inviting me, on the part of the Prince, to be his guest at breakfast to-morrow. I could not go to bed without writing you the good news. Even should I get no sittings, or fail with the portrait, the honour of having breakfast with the Prince will well repay me for my journey.

* * * * *

Sunday, 3.30 p.m..

I have breakfasted with the Prince and Princess Bismarck. We were seven: a Count and his Countess, a doctor from Heidelberg, the Prince's secretary Dr. Chrysander, and myself. A select company, renowned, but not fashionable. We ate scrambled eggs, omelettes, chicken, and brown and white bread; drank Bavarian beer, red wine, and rye whisky.
The Prince is a fine man, very tall and well proportioned, with a good-natured, frank, rosy face, and a head like a baby's, fringed with just a little soft, curly hair.
I was delighted with him. What an idiot I have been not to practise speaking German! I have lost so much of the conversation, and I have no doubt many interesting things were said. The Count talked politics; the Prince of drinking, smoking, and eating—this to me, and in good English; the Princess of pictures, and I gathered that she did not like the new open-air school. After breakfast the Prince smoked a long student's pipe, and told funny stories, the points of which I, of course, lost—but I could gaze at him and take in his colour, and that was all I wanted.

* * * * *

The following is a fragment of a letter, written to my niece, Norah King, the remainder of the letter (eight pages) being lost:—

"... into the breakfast-room, where the Prince, himself, introduced me to his wife and his friends, and we sat down. I sat beside Bismarck, on his left, and facing the Countess, who was on his right. The breakfast was very plain, consisting chiefly of eggs in various forms, with one or two meats.

We drank red wine and beer, and after breakfast a small glass of rye whisky, fifty years old, with our coffee.

"While the coffee was being served the head butler brought a long student's pipe, with a great china bowl well stuffed with tobacco, which, the Prince having adjusted it in his mouth, was lighted by the young Countess. For an hour he sat smoking, talking, jesting—now in English to me, again in German to his other guests, and all the while I envied you your German. When you meet Bismarck how pleased he will be to hear you speak his own beloved tongue.

"On taking leave, the doctor and the Count and Countess were warmly embraced and kissed on both cheeks, and as I stood looking on, I wondered whether the Prince would do the same to me, but he only shook my hand, and said I might come again.

"Two days after I went again, and this time prepared to make a drawing in pastel. Count Herbert Bismarck and his young wife had just arrived from Switzerland, where they had been spending their honeymoon. We sat down en famille. I was the only stranger. This time the conversation was almost all in English—save when private affairs were being discussed—Count Herbert and his wife being ready and fluent in the language.

"The little Princess looked very sweet and gentle, and wore a plain gray walking dress. Count Herbert is rough and ready, and although he was talkative and agreeable to me, I can easily imagine that his reputation for rudeness is well founded.

"Before breakfast I had asked the butler to have my pastels and paper all ready, and as soon as the pipe was lighted I drew back my chair and commenced the drawing. The Prince puffed his pipe, read the newspapers, made comments now and again to the Princess, and sometimes marked passages with an enormous lead pencil, which had been brought to him by one of the servants. I worked about an hour, when the Prince rose, asked to see the sketch, made a criticism or two, and then wished me good-bye. By this time you can imagine that I was in a great state of excitement, and trembling with nervousness. I was very pleased as well, for I had my sketch.

"The next morning, very early, I left Kissingen, rushed along the Rhine to Cologne, through Belgium to Bruxelles, and the day following arrived at Wimereux."

The foregoing letters, to my wife and my niece, Norah, do not contain any reference to an incident which occurred on the second day I visited the Prince, before we sat down to breakfast. Some of the letters may have disappeared; the first eight pages of the one written to Norah are gone. I may have felt some little delicacy in relating a scene which, at the time, may have been more or less wounding to my amour propre—a sentiment which weakens with age, and, in my own case, has almost entirely faded away. This incident, or really scene, remains almost undimmed in my memory. It was so unusual and so startling, that it has been deeply imprinted upon the tissue of my mind, and nothing will ever efface it.

When I arrived at the Schloss, I was shown up to the long, large salon, with great windows at each end—the one in front opening upon a balcony facing the street and court, the other overlooking a stretch of gardens and park, in the direction of the baths where the Prince was then taking the cure.

The door at which I entered led me into the front part of the room. At first no one seemed to be in the room; but on looking at the window, heavily shaded with curtains, at the far end, there appeared the dark contour of a slight and frail woman, motionless and expectant. I understood. It was the Princess, watching and waiting for the Prince, the great and powerful man who was stricken in spirit and in body.

All was deathly still. I stood riveted to the floor, lest I should disturb the watcher. It was pathetic to note the apprehension expressed in the bend of that frail figure as she strained her eyes for the first glimpse of the Prince's carriage leaving the gates of the Kursaal. Presently the horses appeared, glittering in the sunlight, and a distant sound of shouting came, like a sullen murmur, through the window, growing louder and louder as the carriage rapidly neared the castle, and ending in a tumult of deafening noise under the window as the Prince descended from the carriage and hurriedly entered the doorway.

He came at once to the salon to greet the Princess, who had come forward to meet him. On seeing me he drew himself up, frowning, and waited for me to speak. Stepping forward, I said I had come to pay my respects, and added that as he had been kind enough to invite me to come again, I had hoped he would be indulgent enough to grant my request for a sitting.

At this he thundered out, "It is true, I did ask you to come again, but not for a sitting. Is it not enough to be besieged by all these people outside, that you should also come to bother me? I have come here for quiet and rest, to take the cure. Listen to that shouting! They want me to speak to them." At this the Princess went to him and, laying her hand gently on his arm, said, "Only say one word to them, or even show yourself on the balcony, and then they will go away." The noise outside was deafening. Through the din I had heard his voice in stentorian tones, asking why I had come to bother him. His great form towered above me. Resentment had brought the blood to his face, that from pink had turned to red, and from red to purple. His eyes bulged from their sockets, round and blazing, and his contracted brows had thrown the long, stiff hairs of his eyebrows, bristling straight out, like quills.

At the touch of the Princess he relaxed and relented. Going slowly to the window, leaning heavily on his cane, he stepped to the balcony. The hochs poured into the window, louder and louder; bands played, trumpets blared, and in this pandemonium of sound I waited, wondering. I am not a hero-worshipper, and do not fear men. I admire great men. Under the frown of this giant I was perfectly calm. When he returned I bowed, and after expressing a sincere regret for being the cause of any additional pain or annoyance to him, turned and, bowing to the Princess, left the room and the castle. As I was hurrying through the doorway to the street, a voice calling me by name caused me to turn, and I saw, running behind me, Dr. Chrysander, who on joining me said, "Mr. Hamilton, you must come back; the Prince will be very angry if you leave the castle without first breakfasting." To this I replied, with indignation, for although I sympathized entirely with the Prince's outraged feelings, a rising sense of disappointment and displeasure had overcome me, "Breakfast! Why, I did not come all the way from London to breakfast with Prince Bismarck. I came to paint him." "That is all very well," returned the Doctor, "but the Prince will consider it a great breach of hospitality if you go away without breakfast—he will be very angry with me." "But," I interposed, "how can I sit down with the Prince after he has spoken to me as he has just done?" "Oh! that is nothing; but rules of hospitality are very important." So I was led back, and prepared to join the family at table.

The Prince then explained to me that he had given sittings for a portrait only once. At the time of the occupation of Paris by the German troops, the American ambassador, Mr. Washburne, had done some service to the Germans which required the recognition of the Emperor. Bismarck was instructed to offer a decoration to Mr. Washburne, but the ambassador told him that members of the American Diplomatic Corps were prohibited from accepting decorations from other governments. "But we must do something for you: what shall it be? What would you like?" "I should like better than anything else your portrait painted by my friend Mr. Healy," answered the ambassador.

"I was obliged to victimize myself, and sit to Mr. Healy," and continuing, he described his many visits to Lenbach, with whom he was on terms of intimate friendship, and said that he had never given Lenbach any sittings for the numerous portraits that had been made by that painter. It is possible that Lenbach may have sketched him frequently, but that was all.

When breakfast was finished, the Princess said quietly to me, "If it will be of any use to you, the Prince will read the newspaper while he smokes, and you may sketch him." I do not know if this had been prearranged between them, or whether it was not an impromptu expression of a gentle will whose veiled commands could not be disobeyed.

Bismarck was a fluent conversationalist. His English was pungent and forcible, and when speaking of his great boarhound he did not hesitate, even before the ladies, to use a language that was interlarded with the technical and realistic jargon of the kennels.

The doctors for the time being had restricted him to a diet of eggs, of which he partook in many styles—scrambled, fried, and in omelettes—consuming at breakfast a prodigious quantity, which measured in dozens might stagger belief. He talked of drinking, of cocktails, and of wines, and told me that his doctor had said that a man might drink, between the ages of twenty and seventy, fifty thousand bottles of champagne without offending the laws of health or the strict rules of temperance! "I may have exceeded that number perhaps, to say nothing of a few other liquors, such as beer and brandy," he confidentially informed me.

We discussed the social problems of England and America. He thought the negro question a very serious matter for America, and did not hesitate to say that the only solution to that would be the re-institution of slavery!

MR ASQUITH

It is probably more than mere imagination to believe that men of the same type follow the same career—that a priori a priest looks like a priest, a soldier a soldier, a lawyer a lawyer, and so on. It is more difficult to believe that men change in facial form and expression in accordance with their manner of life, their trend of thought, or their daily occupation. And it is almost impossible to believe that a man may grow to look like another after many years of close association in the same career, when at its beginning there existed no resemblance between them.

An anatomist may tell you that when the human brain reaches its fifteen-power standard (its maximum growth, at the age of twenty) the cranium, or bone box that contains it, will not grow more. It delights me, lover of inequality that I am, to inform the anatomist that there is no standard at all for a few exceptional brains, that they go on increasing the number of the cells of the cerebrum until, at a great age, physical decay begins; and, in order to accommodate these new cells, the cranium itself expands and grows.

This expansion and growth in the size of the head is more marked, perhaps, in successful statesmen and politicians than in other men. Herbert Spencer attributes success to the strength of our emotions. I do not know if statesmen are more emotional than other men, but from a study of their heads, in conjunction with my observation of the kind of mental activities required of them, I should say that an intensive cultivation of memory and of memory cells gives the explanation for the growth of the head, and in part explains their success.

Artists and scientists, who generally have small heads and small brains, must not take up their cudgels at this, because an instant's reflection should reassure them. Memory is not reason; memory is merely a collection of objects and images stored away for use. The collection may be interesting and amusing, but it is only like a jumble of carved stones for a Gothic building, of little value until co-ordinated and correlated and cemented together by something more than mere intelligence.

The need for a comprehensive memory is paramount in a man who attains to the dominant position of Prime Minister of England. It is not a debatable assertion that the memory of Mr. Gladstone was and that of Mr. Asquith is surpassingly great, their brains unusually large, and that there was a gradual increase in their size. And it is still more remarkable that I have seen pictures of the two statesmen that bear a kind of resemblance to each other, although there is no resemblance between the two men.

Mr. Asquith appears to me to be more human than Mr. Gladstone. This may be considered a compliment to both men in proportion to the quality of the meaning attached to the word by the reader. But the position they have both occupied among men was so much above the others that any close judgment upon their respective characters will have to be rendered when time shall have placed them among the few other figures in history of equal stature.

At "The Wharf" Mr. Asquith showed only the human side. There he was the man among men—affable, kindly, full of bonhomie, and intensely interested in the real things of life. He made an admirable sitter, complying graciously with every desire, and never for a moment showed a sign of fatigue, or of a wish to be somewhere else.

Although the moment was an historic one, as Mrs. Asquith's Autobiography was about to appear, life proceeded with unruffled calm, and Lucy, Mrs. Asquith's sister, and I painted in peace, under the interested eye of "Margot" herself.

MRS ASQUITH

THERE is a fascinating sound about "The Wharf." It carries one to so many places at once. It recalls sun-sprinkled water, lapping against barnacle-covered posts upholding rickety structures in ancient wood, over which boyish figures hang to peer into clear depths for crawling creatures and lazy fish. It reminds one of rushing noises, of bright colours, of groanings and grindings, as great side-wheel steamers labour and surge before they are rope-bound to giant wooden stays, to empty out the motley throng of joyous and care-free people seeking holiday. So when I first heard that I was to come to "The Wharf," my imagination pictured many things by sea and lake and river, without hitting once upon the place it really is. But more definite names at last led me to think of the Thames and Oxford, and all that charming country that I learned to know so well when Abbey was painting, at Morgan Hall, in Fairford, the Search for the Holy Grail. I could picture Joseph of Arimathea and Guinevere and Launcelot, and all the knights around King Arthur's table. And here, too, had been my son, with Professor Turner, numbering stars that were as grains of sand upon the sea-shore.

And when I found "The Wharf," there was a river and a weir, and the most delightful of houses, a garden full of roses, a mill, a mill-race, and a vine-covered barn—but no wharf!

And then a lady came tripping in to greet me, smiling so frankly and kindly, that I was at home at once, and in love with the books and flowers, and the gay vista, through the garden to the silver willows, casting shadows on the placid river. And, as I stood by her side talking about the simple and pretty border-flowers, I glanced sidewise at the slight, frail, but somewhat rigid figure, at the delicate Dante-like profile, the dark, full eyes, and wondered at the woman who had jumped into the field of life, and surmounted its obstacles at a run, a gallop, a canter, and a trot, but never at a walk. Was she thinking of the flowers, the bees, and the butterflies? Or, like mine, were her thoughts straying among the other thoughts that were then crowding around her—impulses in the ether, surging over her from the most distant lands in the far-flung Empire, because she had revealed her soul to the peoples?

ARTHUR JAMES BALFOUR

MY first sight of Mr. Balfour was at the inauguration of Princes' Club, Knightsbridge, playing tennis. His attitude was an attendant one; he seemed to wait for the ball to do something, rather than to attack it and make it do his will. And this has been his attitude throughout life. It is exemplified by a story told by Mrs. Drew: On their way down to dinner, on the great staircase of Mr. Gladstone's house in Carlton House Terrace, Mr. Balfour paused on the top, where the stairs divide, and, turning to Mrs. Drew, said, "Is there any reason why we should go down on the left rather than the right side?"

It will be remembered how he argued upon the silver question, brought forward by William Jennings Bryan, taking the ground that there might be two sides to that, and thereby puzzling the public and prolonging the controversy. In Margot's Autobiography, Dr. Jowett comments critically upon this attitude in one of his letters.

Men who golf much can never make up their minds, usually hold no opinion upon serious things, and assume that life, religion, and politics are like golf, an uncertain and unsteady game. Their mentality is in strong contrast to that of sportsmen who shoot big or small game. This sort of sport requires instant decision and action, and it has everything to do with the formation of character. It is, of course, unnecessary to remark that men are born golfers, and, like poets, they cannot help themselves.

As for the portrait of Mr. Balfour, I cannot say whether I have painted him or not. He appeared to sit reluctantly, almost unwillingly. His manner, attitude, and expression changed from that of ease and charm, which so conspicuously distinguish him in society, to one of abandoned resignation to an unpleasant operation. While admitting that sitting for one's portrait is not so pleasant as many other things, it can be made an opportunity for rest, and even of entertainment, by the exercise of a little goodwill, and particularly by a more considerate disposition towards the painter. Men are too prone to assume that the artist holds an ambiguous position among citizens. When I write "citizens" I wish it distinctly to be understood that the word is not used as the Socialists use it.

Politicians, soldiers, lawyers, and priests consider themselves to be the mainstay of civilization, whereas it will be found, if history be correctly examined, that they are often the instruments of destruction, while artists have ever been the builders of civilization. Lawyers and priests deal with the accidents of life. Art is concerned with realities. History makes too much of the soldier and the statesman, and too little of the artist. A great tapestry is a record of real achievement in the realm of beauty that surpasses the most eloquent tribute of words to the deeds of kings.

I tried hard to paint Mr. Balfour, but somehow he managed to elude me. And a strange thing happened. All painters are conscious of the phases of a portrait as it grows on the canvas, how it resembles in turn each and every member of the family of the person painted. I once knew a man who painted all his sitters with just a suspicion of himself in each. A portrait of a well-known London doctor looked so much like a German that he was asked if he were of German blood. "No," he replied, "but that portrait was painted by a German."

These examples do not explain the strange happening to Mr. Balfour's portrait. It suddenly began to look like his secretary, Mr. Short. The nose, especially, took the form of the secretary's nose. Almost in affright I tried to alter it, but could not, and by dint of looking Mr. Balfour began to look like Mr. Short. The two men were not at all alike—one was short, the other tall. They both wore small moustaches, the only point of resemblance. I have sometimes noticed, however, that a secretary, either consciously or unconsciously, will imitate a man he admires—in gait, manner, voice, and the dressing of the hair or the cut of the collar.

When the sitting was over I went into the adjoining room and talked with Mr. Short, and while I talked examined him closely to see if he might by a rare chance bear any likeness to Mr. Balfour. I found, to my chagrin, that he was not unlike the picture, but not a bit like Mr. Balfour. I have never known where to attach the blame these coincidences—upon myself, or Mr. Short, or Mr. Balfour. But I never returned to finish the work—it remains as it then was.

I have always admired Mr. Balfour for his unchanging conservatism, his persistent unionism, and his British patriotism. The great shock of August 1914 seemed to unhinge most minds among leaders in the nations. The majority, in the peoples themselves, stood the shock and met it with resolution and courage. Mr. Balfour led them eloquently and untiringly until he met Mr. Wilson in America. From that time there rose in front of him a double staircase, and he is still wondering whether he should go down on the left side or up on the right. This was my opportunity to avenge myself for the failure of the portrait, and to express the resentment I harboured against him for his cavalier treatment of the artist, and I wrote him a few letters on the political situation.

Ever since and even before the end of the Napoleonic wars it has been a characteristic of the English race to ignore the possibility of another great war. The colonists of America prior to the Revolution, and after the conquest of the French and their Indian allies in Canada, settled down peacefully to develop the land. In disregard of the murmurs of discontent against the Crown Government, the people remained to the last unprepared for the impending struggle for independence, and it was only when the Government sent over soldiers to enforce a taxation that was thought to be unreasonable, that the colonists hastily armed themselves for an unequal struggle against trained troops. We know that the inefficiency, in every respect save one—the knowledge derived from the Indians of rough, backwoods fighting—in the meagre armies of General Washington, caused that unfortunate campaign to be prolonged for seven years. Had the colonists been prepared as they should have been, the Crown forces would most probably have been driven from the country, without much loss to either side, in a few months, or less.

In the same country, inhabited principally at that time by people of so-called Anglo-Saxon blood, or where the institutions and habits of the English influenced all the others, certain disputes between the Northern and Southern States, concerning commerce and slavery, became so acute, from the years 1850 to 1860, that war between the two factions was almost openly discussed. The Government at Washington had no army or navy sufficient to quell a rebellion of the Southern States, and regardless of the heat of the discussions on the question of slavery, both in public and in private, the Government made no attempt to strengthen its arm. The fatal hour struck, and in an instant two imperfectly equipped armies faced each other and fought a disastrous fight for four long years. If the Central Government had been prepared, as it should have been, with an adequate army and navy, the rebellion could have been crushed in its infancy, and lives innumerable and property saved.

Nature and the Designer of nature may consider these long wars that deplete and desolate necessary to a mysterious and preconceived plan of life. I remember Senator Stewart once telling me that he had said in a speech to the Senate that no nation had ever become great until after it had had a great war, and that no senator present had been able to deny it. Be that as it may, the want of preparation prolongs the misery and increases the disasters of war, and who knows how many conflicts might be averted by a preponderating strength in one or in several allied nations?

In 1870 France thought she was prepared, but was not. But her adversary, Germany, was ready, and the struggle was short and comparatively bloodless.

A few months after the first Boer War I was sitting in the Art Club of Philadelphia with Mr. William Addicks, Mr. Harrison Morris, and two or three other men, who were discussing the short and ineffective conflict that had left President Krüger master of the situation in Africa. Mr. Addicks, brother of the notorious aspirant to represent Delaware in the Senate, had just returned from England, where he had been a guest at several country houses, and he was recounting the various views upon the rights and wrongs of the situation he had heard from his English friends, ending by saying, with great satisfaction, that "Oom Paul had been too clever for the British, who were easily hoodwinked." There was a consensus of opinion that the Boers had rightly won, and that the affair was finished. I rose to go, and said quietly, "It is not settled; there will be and must be another war. It may come in two or in ten years, but England must be paramount in Africa."

My point is this: that if I could foresee another war, why did not the British Government, with all the means at its disposal for obtaining information, foresee it and prepare for it? I am expressing no sympathy and taking no sides, but though we may neither approve nor disapprove of the "flu," when it first shows itself it is as well to provide a nurse and a doctor.

All this has nothing to do with portrait painting. Mr. Balfour would have nothing to do with it, so I determined to challenge him in his own field—to him I was, of course, invisible.

Years after the episode in the club, the second Boer War had begun. A party of men were shooting partridges over the picturesque hills of Pembrokeshire—a member of Parliament, his brother, a local justice of the peace, a retired Indian colonel, a master of foxhounds, and myself. The member said, "This war will not be over so soon as the Government expects." "No," I replied, "they don't know how to fight it, and are not prepared." And continuing, for no one demurred, "If Lord Salisbury would send for Buffalo Bill, and tell him to gather together thirty thousand cowboys, and supply him with plenty of horses, guns, and ammunition, he would settle it in three months." This was received with murmurs of expostulation and dissent, the colonel's voice being the loudest. But after a thoughtful silence he said, "It could not be done, but I believe you are right."

The Boers' tactics were to fight and run; the cowboys would have run after them and probably caught them.

On returning to London I became seriously alarmed at the situation, and saw Edward Clifford, of the Church Army, who was an old and intimate friend of George Wyndham, the Secretary for War. I asked him to see Mr.

Wyndham and urge upon him the necessity for sending at least forty thousand men to Africa. I wrote a letter for him to read to Mr. Wyndham, quoting from American history the methods of fighting that sort of guerrilla warfare always adopted by the colonists, and later by the Federal cavalry, when dealing with Indians. Clifford replied that they, the Government, would know their business best. They knew it so well that, in the end, more than three hundred thousand men were sent fourteen thousand miles in ships to conquer, with great difficulty, roving bands of about sixteen thousand farmers.

Between 1870 and 1914 repeated warnings were given that Germany was increasing her army, and perfecting its equipment and drill for a war. She was also building a powerful navy; and it was pointed out that it could only be intended for use against Great Britain's navy. German writers openly avowed this intention. Some one has written that "God made the English navy, and man made the army." As a matter of fact the army was not made at all. When the vain monarch, half-crazed with blinding ambition, attacked Russia, France, and Belgium, the English navy, by God's will, was ready; but the brave little army, type of the best that England had of chivalrous and knightly men, was hopelessly outnumbered on the plains of France and Flanders.

Mr. Balfour was a member of the Government, or sitting on the Opposition Benches all the time!

One is almost forced to the conclusion that English-speaking peoples consider it a virtue to be unprepared for war. Several sentiments may be discovered underlying this almost unique position among the nations—pride, an undue sense of security, pacifism, religious scruples—but, whatever the sentiment may be, it is responsible, as most sentiments are, for many cruel mistakes.

When the Government of the United States tardily decided to enter into the war, an army had to be raised. Mr. Balfour went over to Washington to warn the American Government against the mistakes that had been made in England. His warning did not prevent similar blunders. Unsuitable men were enrolled, camps were located in unhealthy positions, nothing was promptly provided for the comfort of the recruits, many died from exposure and insufficient food. There were neither sheds, nor tents, nor blankets, nor clothing, nor arms. These are the inevitable fruits of unpreparedness.

Ambassadors still live under the impression that the delegates of a democratic and self-ruling people can speak as sovereigns. Mr. Balfour went to Washington and mixed with members of Mr. Wilson's Cabinet, and with the Diplomatic Corps, and other exalted personages. He did not read the newspapers, and he did not gather information from the people themselves as to what they were thinking. The people knew that the Senate of the

United States would not agree to the Treaty of Versailles, nor be a party to the League of Nations. I wrote this to Mr. Balfour, and pointed out what Mr. Davis, Mr. Wilson's ambassador to London, did not do, when he addressed the Oxford Union, viz. that the Constitution of the United States gave no power of independent action to the President in making treaties, but defined and limited his power in a short sentence: "The President may make treaties by the advice, and with the consent, of the Senate."

The Senate was not asked for its advice, and—but not for that reason only—refused its consent. The Senate understood the people, and the people acknowledged that understanding by electing a republican to succeed Mr. Wilson. No one in Paris or in London seemed to understand the situation; no one seemed to consider whether Mr. Wilson represented the whole of the American people or not. In all probability they did not know that Mr. Wilson originally was a minority President, that he owed his election to a split in the Republican Party, and to the skilful management of the election campaign by "Colonel" House, who had a large part in its success.

When the League of Nations held its sittings under the presidency of Mr. Balfour, I again wrote him that the Senate of the United States would not accept the League, or ratify the Treaty of Versailles, that the Senate had been flouted, and its privileges challenged. Unlike the House of Lords, that had divested itself of its powers, the Senate was determined to maintain the position granted to it under the Constitution, and to exercise its right of rejecting a treaty; and in view of this any position taken up by the League in council might have to be modified, in case of the advent of a republican President.

The new Government at Washington has already interfered with the mandates of the League, and I may safely say now that it will in the future treat the League, should it set itself up as a super-government, in the same way as it will treat any other government or nation, questioning its orders or mandates, should they appear in any way to affect the interests of the American people.

It may be recalled that Lord Curzon once said, in the House of Commons, that "it was no part of the duty of a Minister of the Crown to anticipate events." But even in that case the privilege may still be permitted to an ordinary pedestrian to carry an umbrella in April!

CARDINAL MANNING

I SUCCEEDED in obtaining a drawing in pastel of Cardinal Manning which I was induced to part with to the Pennsylvania Academy of the Fine Arts, to my great regret, and which I have offered to repurchase.

The Cardinal was one of my best and most amiable sitters. While I worked, he read his breviary, or chatted with me upon many of the social and economic topics of the day. How futile such discussions are can only be realized after a lapse of twenty years, when changes have taken place that alter radically one's conception of details—the underlying principles only remaining unchanged.

Cardinal Manning was a tall, picturesque ecclesiastic, very careless in dress, with an exceedingly small face but a wide and prominent forehead. On one occasion when he was lecturing, he told me, a man up in the gallery, looking down upon him, and seeing his face foreshortened, called out in a voice that he and all could hear, "Why, he has no face; he's all forehead!"

"The only time a man should look in a mirror is when he is shaving," the Cardinal continued; and I thought to myself that, in his case, to avoid the sin of vanity, he considered once a week sufficient. He did not look on the reverse of the picture; for some people suffer agonies of remorse and self-abasement when they look into mirrors.

The Cardinal did not consider sitting for a portrait so vain an act as looking into a mirror. He consented to be painted with great goodwill, and enlivened the hours by anecdotes of paintings and painters. There were three kinds of portrait painters, he thought—those who paint you as they think they see you, those who paint you as they think they ought to see you, and those who paint you as you are. He had given sittings to George F. Watts, who belonged to the second class, and who had painted him "as he thought he ought to do."

JOHN TYNDALL

JOHN TYNDALL was one of that remarkable group of scientists who dragged Truth from her hiding-place and exposed her, shrinking, to the astonished gaze of gaping multitudes. Falsehood, like all vicious, brazen things, shrieked her shrill protest: Darwin, Huxley, and Tyndall, standing shoulder to shoulder, stoutly defended the new-found Truth from the vicious attacks of the vixen and her votaries.

John Tyndall was the freest, frankest, and most open-minded man I have ever met. Épanouissement, the act of opening out, expresses his nature better than any English word I can think of. He met you and greeted you like the fresh, pine-scented breeze that blows over his beloved hills of Hindhead.

Tyndall built himself two nests—one on Hindhead, overlooking the Devil's Punch Bowl, the other far up on the high Alps. It was in the latter place that he made the experiments which determined that life is not due to spontaneous generation, that where no life is, no life can be derived; and there for many years he passed the summers, climbing the peaks that rose from the snows and glaciers of the Matterhorn. He built the house which became his permanent home among the heather and pines of that high range of hills that receive the last breath of the sea winds as they pass northward from the English Channel over the downs that overlook the Isle of Wight.

He loved to be isolated with Nature. When Tyndall first went to Hindhead there were no houses on that bleak bit of moorland, no human folk, save a few wandering gipsies, to remind him of the existence of coal-sodden cities. The air was not polluted with unburnt carbon, and there was no veil of grey smoke, which the ignorant call fog, to dim the horizon that outlined, in clear-cut purple masses, the changing skies that gave him, night and day, a spectacle always sublime and often magnificent. Here he could walk, unseen by other men, on the dry sand of the hill-tops, and study the creatures that burrowed in it, or the wild plants that matted its surface. But this dream of bliss, of splendid isolation in Nature's solitudes, was soon to be disturbed and turned into a nightmare.

By building a house in the distant haunts of Nature's wild things Tyndall had unwittingly advertised the spot, and its unquestioned purity of air. Instead of purchasing a sufficiently large tract of land to ensure his isolation, he confined himself to a moderate acreage, never for a moment thinking that anyone would come to such a lonely place. When it was too late to correct his error of judgment, he one day discovered workmen constructing a house within two hundred yards of his windows and immediately on the other side of the boundary of his property. He spared no effort to dissuade the new-corner from his design, but without avail. In a few weeks' time he found the view from his southern windows and from his garden blemished by the roof of a suburban-like villa, and, what was really far more disturbing to him, his sense of isolation gone. He now did something that to me seemed perfectly natural—he caused to be built a large screen, to imitate in its contour the appearance of growing pine-trees, and he fringed the sides with pine-branches to give it the effect of reality. He also planted small pines and firs around the screen and along the edge of his property to form natural barriers against the invasion of oncoming villas, for they began to multiply rapidly. Viewed from the road approaching Hindhead the screen was an eyesore, and it caused a feeling of irritation among the good people of Haslemere who were in the habit of making excursions to the Devil's Punch Bowl. The screen was only remarkable because of the place, for similar shields of all sorts are put up in the gardens and parks of great estates every day without exciting any comment. Mrs. Tyndall gave me a long history of the transaction, and she aroused my sympathy and my indignation against the neighbour; for had he possessed a grain of neighbourly behaviour in his nature, he would have selected another spot just as good for his house, and out of view of Tyndall's.

This love of solitude which appeals so strongly to certain temperaments recalls a vivid imagination of my boyhood. The desire to be alone was so strong within me, that my idea of perfect happiness was to live in a planet all my own. I can now recall these visions of a time when I could see myself "paddling my own canoe" on a placid river overhung with flower-bearing trees and fruit-laden vines, where the stillness was broken only by the voices of birds. And if Edgar Allan Poe's theory, as explained by Agathos to Einos, be true, that motion creates, and that the source of all motion is thought, who may gainsay that my boyish thought may not have created a planet somewhere in space that is to receive me in the evermore? How often have I sought the solitude of the forest with my gun, where the mysterious and whispering music of insects was broken only by the occasional whirring of the partridge, and where I lingered in its depths until the last rays of the sun have warned me, by their deep red glow on the bark of leafless trees, that night would overtake me if I did not retrace my paths and seek the protection of humankind. On several different occasions Nature has seemed to reveal to my eyes alone spectacles of entrancing splendour that she would not grant to less discerning faculties, lest her chastity be outraged by imperfect worship; and so I found myself in complete harmony with the sentiments of this great thinker and dreamer of Hindhead.

I lived at "The Hut" near by while I was painting the portrait of Tyndall. One day at dinner a guest at the inn, who was sitting not far from me, on the same side of the table, handed me a glass with a yellow liquid in it, and asked me what it was, saying that he had ordered ginger beer, but that there seemed to be something wrong with it. After a whiff at the glass, I replied that most men would think that there was something right about it, because it was whisky. "Oh my!" he replied, "I'm a teetotaller, and I have drunk nearly all of it; it is a large glass, and it was full." "And that is what you will be, I should think, very shortly," I replied.

Noticing something very familiar in his face, I asked him if he happened to be Dr. Porter, of Philadelphia. "No," he replied, "I have never been to America, but at the same time I know you." "Well," said I, "if you are not Dr. Porter, whom you strangely resemble, I cannot imagine how you can know me." "I have been in your house—Alpha House—to see you about your portrait of Mr. Gladstone. You permitted me, afterwards, to introduce it in a volume of his speeches that I was editing. My name is Hutton."

While I lived at "The Hut" I lunched daily with the Professor and Mrs. Tyndall. Professor Tyndall had been suffering for a long time from insomnia. He had discovered, he thought, in the peculiar tissue of calf's head and tripe a narcotic principle of sufficient strength to compose him for sleep. This formed the staple of his diet, and the dishes were prepared under the supervision of Mrs. Tyndall, whose devotion to her husband amounted to idolatry.

At that time an invalid, Tyndall passed the day in a dressing-gown, reclining for the greater part of it on a couch in one of the libraries. I regret that there is no record of his conversation, for he was a fluent and willing talker, eager to instruct or amuse me while I painted. He touched frequently upon belief and unbelief, and I often seemed to detect a kind of apology for his attitude of "I don't know." He was not so uncompromising in his attitude as Darwin, who, one day after a long discussion upon religion at table, rose from his chair, and throwing his long leg over the back of it and planting his foot firmly down in the seat, said to Tyndall reproachfully, "Why, I believe you still hang on to some shreds of belief!" Tyndall replied that it was not so, but that he was ready to affirm nothing: he had neither proof nor disproof of the existence of God; he simply did not know. It was at this time that the controversy on miracles between Gladstone and Huxley was at its height, and the subject was uppermost with a good many people. To my query, "Don't you think the need of a God is so strong in the mind of the race, that the mere desire itself would assume such force and volume that it would create a Providence?" He replied by quoting Napoleon's saying, "If there had not been any God, men would certainly have had to invent one."

In the library one day, while I was painting and he was talking on the same subject, he swept his arm around the room, and said, "You must not think that I speak without knowledge of the subject—that, like many who simply say 'I do not believe,' I have not studied it. Look at the titles of these books; all, or almost all, in this room are works on religion. I have made myself master of the thought of theologians of all times and of all creeds. I do not speak idly and ignorantly." Such was the point of view of the scientist. Every rational mind must agree with the deductions drawn from an investigation of natural processes, yet the wisdom of men may possibly be foolishness to God. Tyndall held that there was no such thing as absolute truth, that all things seemed to possess two qualities—activity and change. What the final activity and the final change may be who can tell?

A Hair, they say, divides the False and True;
Yes; and a single Alif were the clue,
Could you but find it, to the Treasure-house,
And peradventure to the Master too;

Whose secret Presence, through Creation's veins
Running, Quicksilver-like eludes your pains:
Taking all shapes from Máh to Máhi; and
They change and perish all—but He remains.

Not long ago I asked a young man who had been a Presbyterian, and who had gone over to Rome with the intention of becoming a monk—he has not yet put on the cowl—if there was any proof to be given in favour of agnosticism, of unbelief. He answered, "None." I then asked, "Is there any real proof of the Divinity of Christ?" and he answered, "None." On referring him to the strange fact of the conversion of St. Paul, he said, "That may have been an illusion." I merely remarked that these were unlooked-for answers from a Roman Catholic. However, if the essence of faith is a belief in things unseen, his answers could not have been different. Yet "I know that my Redeemer liveth" is not said idly by multitudes of sane men and women.

There are still a good many things that we know nothing about—water is one and life is another. The two, as a matter of fact, are inseparable—life cannot exist without water. Of all the emotions there are two that differ from the others, and they are inexplicable upon any rational hypothesis. These are Profane and Divine Love. Profane love is common to the animals and man, and is conspicuous as a sentiment among birds. When I speak of love I do not mean lust, or even desire—I mean that emotion which causes two birds to select among thousands a mate: that fidelity which makes the wild grey goose of a certain species to mate but once. The emotion of profane love is identical in its effects with the emotion produced by conversion. It inspires a feeling of goodwill towards men. In spite of the fact that Seneca has written that love is a disease and a weakness to which no self-respecting man would succumb, it is a matter of knowledge that innumerable strong men of high character have fallen under its spell. No one can truthfully say that St. Paul was a dreamer, a visionary, or a fool. He plainly says that he was stricken suddenly, and became a convert to the truth of God. His life was changed from that moment. His story is the story of numberless men and women of good sense and repute in all Christian Churches. This is a matter for students of mind. Here are two emotions of the mind as mysterious as life itself. The searchers for the origin of life should not arrogate to themselves too much—they should wait until they know what life is, what thought is, and what emotion is. And they are still a long way off. "Can ye by seeking find out God?"

It is not a little remarkable that astronomers are religious men, and believers in a Divine direction of this vast universe, while scientists who deal with fossils and with biology are incredulous, and as a rule unbelievers. A knowledge of little things seems to be also a dangerous thing. One man looks out of a window and sees mud, another looks out and sees stars.

Tyndall took the safe ground, compromising, as it were, between the knowable and the unknowable. What his fearless and reasonable nature would have thought of the present-day creed that MAN is God I dare not consider.

A question of much greater importance to Tyndall at that time than belief and unbelief, and around which the political factions were raging, was Home Rule.

John Tyndall was a loyal Irishman; he understood perfectly the situation in Ireland, a situation which had grown out of the circumstances of its history. He knew that however unfortunate those circumstances may have been during the long centuries of the island's evolution, they had their origin in the turbulent character of the original peoples, and however unjust or unfair may have seemed to be the actions of the sovereigns of England, that the circumstances were inevitable, and that to give Home Rule to a house divided against itself would not unite it, but still further divide it. Upon this subject he conversed more energetically than upon any other—he was often vehement. At one time an admirer and supporter of Mr. Gladstone, he now had become one of his bitterest political foes. He wrote long letters to The Times, some of them so strong in tone that even that courageous newspaper would not publish them. I became frequently his courier, and carried the letters to London in order that they might reach sooner Printing House Square. Feeling ran higher and higher—one after another, Bright, Hartington, and Chamberlain seceded from the Liberal Party, and the Unionist Party was formed.

Tyndall has long been dead. We cannot know what he would now think of the Unionist Party, what he would think of Carson's surrender, of the acceptance of Home Rule by Ulster, of its probable rejection by the rest of Ireland, of the endless warfare.

Rising to a sitting position on his couch one day, after a more than usually vigorous denunciation of Home Rule, he burst forth, "Old as I am and ill as I am, the strength will be given to me to take that musket," pointing to an old gun on the wall, "and carry it across to Ireland to join the ranks of the loyalists."

Two portraits are the result of my visit to Hindhead. One was presented to the National Portrait Gallery by Mrs. Tyndall, and the other she retained. She thought she gave the best one to the nation, but I preferred the other.

Mrs. Tyndall made my visit agreeable and interesting. We drove to many places in the neighbourhood—to the James' really attractive rock garden, to hear Mr. Jackson play on his great organ.

My friend Walter Tyndale then lived in Haslemere, and I often walked down to the village to see him. He was, and is, an ardent Home Ruler. It was Walter Tyndale who, at the Grey House, Hornton Street, first discussed the question with me, and it was then that I instinctively took the side of Ulster. How could I help it? Two of my grandparents were born near Ballymena, in County Antrim.

HERBERT SPENCER

WHEN I was at Hindhead, painting John Tyndall, the conversation often turned upon Herbert Spencer. On expressing a desire to make his portrait, Mrs. Tyndall said she would ask for sittings for me. She received from Spencer a long letter in reply, giving an infinite number of reasons for refusing to have the portrait done—among others, that some one might want to buy the portrait, whereby he would be unwittingly the cause of financial embarrassment to the purchaser, and of profit to some profligate artist! Mrs. Tyndall would not give me the letter, and I believe has destroyed it, thereby depriving readers of a gem in Spencerian prose and unconscious wit.

I now forget the means I employed to obtain the sittings, but his consent was finally given, and what happened is recorded in the letters I wrote to my wife.

Alpha House,
Regent's Park.
Sunday.

My dear Clara

I am to commence Herbert Spencer to-morrow at eleven, so the trip to Hawarden must be put off until after the 19th.

* * * * *

Saturday.

I had a very good sitting from Spencer yesterday, and I go again to-day. The light is very bad now, and there is a prospect of a black fog, but I keep hoping that it will clear sufficiently to enable me to finish this afternoon.

* * * * *

Tuesday Evening.

You can have no conception of the annoyance which this plague of fleas is giving me. If the powder which Mrs. Evans has scattered on the floors does not soon kill the pests, I shall be driven out of the house by them. Even in the streets I am not safe from their attacks, for they harbour in my clothes, and if I put my hand in my overcoat pocket it is nibbled at once. Yesterday, while painting Mr. Spencer, one of the voracious insects commenced an attack on my wrist, under my cuff, and where I could not dislodge him. I hardly dared to make a great effort to catch him because I was afraid Mr. Spencer would detect me in the act, so I had to suffer the wretch to nip me in twenty places before I could drive him away. Between these vermin and a bad toothache I have had a wretched time since Saturday, but I am better now, so do not mind telling you of my past misfortunes.

Mr. Spencer is old. He strikes me as being a vain man, and though like Professor Tyndall in features, he differs from him very materially in character. He selected Burgess to paint his portrait because Burgess was not a portrait painter; and he explained this apparent inconsistency by saying that he thought the portrait would be more carefully carried out in its details by a man who was not accustomed to paint portraits.

He is formal and precise in manner and speech, but he has a pleasant though not familiar smile. I asked him if he thought the size of the head had anything to do with ability or success in life, and he replied, "No," that I had fallen into a common error of supposing that the brain was the seat of the intellect, whereas it was the seat of the emotions. I was staggered, and asked him what he considered the organ of intelligence, and wondered whether he would name the liver, the lungs, or the heart, but he reassured me by answering that the intelligence resided, of course, in the brain, but that it occupied a very insignificant part as compared with the emotions; and then he stopped me, saying that he could not discuss anything of a serious nature because of his ill-health, that our conversation must be entirely gossipy. After an interval of silence, during which he asked whether he might be permitted to close his eyes, he reverted to the question by saying, "You, of course, do not mean that a large head is always a sign of intellectual capacity, and that a small one is not," and on my replying in the negative, he added, "No doubt size has something to do with the quantity or quality of the intellect, but achievement depends upon the emotions!" "Then I was right," said I, "when I once said to my doctor that I believed that the affections and all the moral faculties had their origin in the sense of touch." Looking at me quickly and sharply, he said, "What a heterogeneous idea!" and then, impatiently, "But I must not discuss. You have no idea how sensitive my mind is to all outside influence. I have ear-stoppers which I sometimes use to prevent the noise of conversation. I cannot see even my most intimate friends because of my illness." I painted on until half-past twelve, when he asked to be relieved, promising to be ready earlier the next morning. He left the room with a formal bow, but after a time returned to ask a question concerning my stay in town, and then shook hands with me in a more cordial manner.

* * * * *

Sunday.

My sitting with Spencer yesterday was amusing and irritating. It appears that he had looked at the portrait and discovered that I had made the upper lip too long. On sitting down to work he commented on this, admitting that his lip was unusually long, and, according to the rule, too long, but that I had made the nose also too short, which only aggravated the matter. "It is also unduly convex and prominent, and although my lip may not be concave and curved inwards, as it should be, it is not so unusually pronounced as you have indicated; in fact—in a final burst—"you have made it look like a gorilla's!"

This almost unnerved me, but I went to work, and, seeing that I had made the nose a trifle too short, I lengthened it, but it was not enough for the savant. He, at the end of the sitting, insisted on having a quarter of an inch of flesh colour added to the nose, so that it might be dry to work over on Monday, and I mildly but firmly refused to do this outrageous thing.

On the previous sitting we had been conversing about painters losing their health by overwork: at least Spencer mentioned that Frank Holl had died from overwork, that Leighton was now broken down from over-attention to his work, as were several others, like Calderon and Burgess. I admitted that it might be so, although there had been many instances of painters reaching a very ripe old age under the stimulus of work, and that it was generally through avarice that they broke down, and consequently were not to be pitied.

We touched, then, upon Millais and his wealth and his house, which reminded Spencer of a remark of Carlyle's, on entering the hall of Millais' house: "What! has all this been produced by painting pictures? Then men are greater fools than I thought them." "Yes, I have sometimes thought as Carlyle," I replied, "for in some of my moods I have said that the daubing of little spots of paint on canvas, in imitation of the things around us, is the most foolish of all the foolish ways of spending a life. Yet, on the other hand, is not Art—sculpture, architecture, painting, etc.—the ultimate aim of existence, the grandest and most entrancing of all our pursuits? The wealthy and the leisured classes go to Art as the highest and final enjoyment of existence, even those who do not understand it."

"Not so," said Spencer; "it is only another means of distinction. When men fail to make themselves celebrated, they think to make themselves distinguished by their possessions." "But," said I, "referring again to Carlyle, is not literature a form of art?" "That," he replied, "depends on the kind of literature." "Is not Sartor Resartus an artistic work?" I asked. "Yes," he answered, "it is an artistic rendering of a philosophic idea."

Then he fell foul of the Old Masters, on my referring to Franz Hals and his style, saying that every age thought the preceding one better, and that even the Iliad was full of complaints of the degeneracy of man. Spencer had led up to this by expressing a regret that there existed no means of marking a picture so as effectually to prevent imitation and forgery, referring, I believe, to the portrait of himself by Burgess. I had replied that the style was the only true indication of the authenticity of a work, and even that could not be depended upon when the style was obscure, undecided, or commonplace.

Yesterday he reverted again to the Old Masters, with more than usual bitterness, accused them of puerility and many other faults, said they never made reflections in their shadows, but carried them around a limb or an object with increasing darkness, until in the end they were blacker than black. In fact, that they did not understand reflected lights.

I said that I had been taught to ignore reflections in the shadows, and that once, having made a drawing with transparent shadows, the professor rubbed them out, telling me that I must not see them. "What incompetent fool was that?" Spencer demanded. I went on to say that the result of this teaching had been to make me a painter of reflected light, and that I painted nearly all my portraits in shadow with the face illumined by a book or paper. This amused him, and he laughed heartily.

He went on to say that his opinion was considered a heresy, but that Calderon had in part upheld him, for he (Calderon) had once said that men went daft when they talked of the Old Masters. I suggested Velasquez. Spencer announced that he was "stiff, strained, and awkward"; that Raphael owed his reputation to the religion in his works—that always took; that Van Eyck's John Arnolfini and Wife was an ugly thing; that photography had helped men to perceive the just relation and proportion of shadows, etc., etc. The drapery of the old Greeks was a farce, Spencer declared, adding that it looked as though it had been dipped in water to make it cling around the form. On my replying that it had, he seemed surprised, and laughed again. I then told him that it was a common custom for modern sculptors to do the same. "Then that was an imitation of the Greeks," he commented. I told him that I knew a man (referring to Alfred Gilbert) who rolled his clay out into thin blankets with a piecrust rolling-pin, and then put them around his nude figures, adapting the folds to the body and limbs, as wet cloths would fall into the hollows and cling to the rounded surfaces. All this was nuts for him to crack.

"If that statuette in marble, of Foley's," said Spencer, pointing to the mantel, where something covered with a silk pillow-case stood, "were found now in broken fragments in the Tiber, or in some ruins of ancient Greece, it would be upheld to the world as a miraculous gem." "Did Foley do much work in Rome?" I asked, not venturing upon an opinion as to the merit of his Art compared to that of the ancients.

Finally Spencer expressed surprise at the great reputation which Du Maurier had made for himself by his novels. I admitted that Trilby had had a great success, more particularly in America, where certain of the clergy had attacked it in the religious Press, which only advertised it the more. He then said that it was the habit with a certain set of faddists to assert that men were either all good or all bad, that no good man could do wrong innocently, and so on, which seems a contradiction to what we must perceive by an examination of our own personal desires, motives and actions, and so on. He wondered whether Trilby had been translated into French. I thought it would not suit the French taste, or be understood by the public, that it was too entirely English to be appreciated by that very precise people. Daudet, of course, might understand some of it.

During the sittings Spencer made some ingenious suggestions concerning measurements and tone, by the use of glass screens, which might prove to be of value.

LORD LEIGHTON

WHEN Lord Leighton's portrait was first exhibited, at the Goupil Gallery, I was standing looking at it, beside Joseph Pennell, who said, "I did not know before that he was a Jew." What is frequently concealed in the face itself is often revealed in a portrait. The movement of the muscles over the forms of the bones deceives the observer, but when everything is fixed and still, as in most portraits, the racial characteristics appear. Many have asked me if "General" Booth was a Jew, but I could always reply in the negative, because no trace of Israelitish blood appears in either of the two portraits I painted of him.

Lord Leighton had the talents of the race and all its virtues, even though an almost invisible line of that extraordinary and, shall I say, mystery blood flowed in his veins. He was a courtier, a persuasive orator, a graceful painter, and a forceful sculptor; a man of the world, a man of affairs, and, as President of the Royal Academy, unequalled in administrative ability. As upon George F. Watts, the sun of Italy had glowed upon his ambrosial curls, and he had brought from that home of Art and civilization the divine blessing of the goddess who presides there. Her spirit and influence were ever upon him, and he often left the cold and truly inhospitable climes of Albion to receive new inspiration at her shrine, the only shrine at which he worshipped.

The Jews are, many of them, supersensitive to that which seems to be implied in their race-name. Recently a Lord Chief Justice of England brought the subject up in open court, when counsel happened to say, "A Jew, I suppose?" The Judge asked, "What does that remark imply?" and followed with a lengthy comment upon the improper prejudice likely to be produced upon the mind of a jury by certain tones of voice and other subtleties of innuendo. Counsel, like a wise and prudent man, bowed to the remarks of the Judge, and agreed to a dictum which, if carried to the extreme, would not only lead to useless embarrassment in the conduct of a case, but to a positive fear of offending a judge by referring derogatively to the nationality of his people, were he Scot, Irish, American, or Jew.

What nation, it may be asked, has escaped the implication of ridicule and contempt conveyed in the intonation of its name? And are Christians spared by the Jew or the Mohammedan? The fact is that every people inhabiting this petty globe come under the lash of the scornful and contemptuous tongue of every other people. To be called an American in a rising inflection of the voice today, when Americans stand as the inheritors of all that is highest and noblest in civilization and purest in religious impulses, is more unexpected and unreasonable than to be called a Jew. When all is considered, what has Israel to complain of? Is not its history the history of the human race? Is not its God the God of all the nations of the earth? Is not the Messiah a direct descendant of Abraham and David? If the acquisitiveness of some of its people has caused resentment in the other peoples, that feeling is not ill-founded.

The sketch I made of Henry Irving shows that he was a Jew, and an amusing story connected with this is related in his monograph.

I cannot say that my first impression of Lord Leighton, the day Onslow Ford took me to his house, in Holland Park Road, was favourable to him. He was courteous and affable, but I cannot say he was kindly. Very few people are kindly; and no assumption of that virtue, in face, manner, or tone, will deceive anyone to whom real kindliness is necessary. Many kindly men are, at times, distant, cold, forbidding, and rude; in fact, the kind man can be cruel. The man who is proverbially courteous to all, and at all times, is a hollow and selfish mask.

And I did not like his appearance or his dress, the mode of his hair, a certain kind of classical beauty—or imitation of it. The cut of his clothes created the impression that he had no real tradition behind him. At that time—and ever after—Leighton looked upon Whistler as a queer fish, amusing no doubt, but to be suspected, both in his manners and in his Art. The odd part of all this is that the two men, though so entirely different, were alike in their differences. Recalling them now, as two figures, standing side by side, the stamp of complete unconventionality is upon each. Both wore long hair, one in curls, the other in ringlets; one had a white lock, the other white streaks; the hats, coats, trousers, and shoes all differed, but then they differed from all other hats, coats, trousers, and shoes. This unity of purpose, diversely expressed, had a similar impulse in dissimilar minds, the impulse to be artists in everything, even in appearance. Here were two men of similar tastes, who could not savour each other's food. Leighton stood for English respectability, and sought the homage of the great. Whistler, a Bohemian malgré lui, stood for his own Art, and was looked upon as a sort of pariah by Philistines, both high and low.

Time sweeps away the excrescences, reduces all men, not to the forked radishes of Carlyle, but to a bag of bones, any two pairs of which are interchangeable.

Both men left their impression upon the world. The painter Leighton was also a great sculptor. The sketch for the man stretching—"The Sluggard" he called it—is a master-piece, hardly excelled in mediæval or modern Art. If his painting was too conventional, too academic, his design was full of grace and charm, and when he confined himself to such subjects as The Garden of the Hesperides and The Summer Moon he was at home, and could display his full, if limited, power. When he attempted the tragic, he failed. Whistler understood the limitations in Art and in himself, and was content to trifle in a masterly manner with subjects that Leighton would have disdained to consider. But he trifled seriously; his fame will be endless. It is sometimes easier to describe a man by contrasting him with another whose unlikeness is more a matter of degree than of plane.

After several visits to Leighton House I began to like Lord Leighton, and he became more friendly to me. I often wondered if he suspected me because I was an American. Americans do not, as a rule, address Englishmen in America with, "Oh! you're an Englishman!" Why are Americans in England not taken for granted? Among artists they have been fairly numerous and very conspicuous. Benjamin West arrived in London from Philadelphia and became President of the Royal Academy. John Copley, a Bostonian, lived in London and painted portraits. His son, Baron Lyndhurst, became Lord Chancellor of England, and a conspicuous figure. Stuart was a wandering portrait painter in the United Kingdom, and has left there many works that are now of great and increasing value. Leslie and Boughton were both Americans. Of my contemporaries I shall not speak.

Finally I thought that Lord Leighton might be added to the group of portraits of artists I had commenced, so I asked him for sittings. He said he had so little time because he gave all the hours he could spare from his official duties, that involved him in social obligations, to his pictures. But if I would not object to coming early in the morning he would give me an hour or so before breakfast, which he took at half-past ten. Then, without lunching, he had the whole day in the studio until five, when his brougham came, and he drove away.

That suited me perfectly, and I commenced work in a small room overlooking, from a latticed window, the Persian Court below, where the music of a trickling fountain played all day long. These were very happy mornings, and conversation flowed as freely as the fountain over many a field of Art. Now I can recall but one thing: when I mentioned the work of Franz Hals and the characteristic hands he painted, Leighton ejaculated, "Yes, and such hands!"

He told me I was wasting my time painting him.

At half-past ten breakfast was announced, and we went down to the dining-room. He had had his cup of tea at seven, and I could not have had much more, so we were both hungry. The breakfast was laid out in silver dishes on a round table, and by its side, and at Leighton's right hand, there was another smaller table with plates and knives and forks in reserve. There was no servant in attendance. Leighton helped himself and me with great deftness and ease, and passed the first dish, piping hot, across the table, on a hot plate. When the first course was finished we placed the used plates and forks on the reserve table and took fresh plates from it. Now there was one thing about these breakfasts that I shall not forget—the grilled bacon. It surpassed any bacon I have ever seen or tasted, and I can compare it—may the roses forgive me!—only to the pink petals of some rather large and strange rose that had fallen to pieces in the dish. I do not say that it tasted like rose leaves, or smelled either like pot-pourri or attar of roses: and of this I am very glad, because my appetite demanded something less delicately fragrant, and more substantial and nourishing; but it was bacon cured à point, with the right flavour of smoking peat, and cooked lightly and lovingly by some experienced chef de cuisine. The dinners, you ask? Well, they were excellent; but I have had others, the most remarkable of which does not enter here, for I did not paint the host; he was by far too rich to think of having his portrait done.

Those breakfasts were the undoing of the portrait, for from the time I sat down to work I could think of nothing but the coffee and bacon, and I was so constantly on the qui vive for the first word of announcement, or the first faint odour of bacon, which, of course, in that well-regulated establishment, never was allowed to go anywhere but up the chimney, that my work suffered from the persistent distraction, and failed miserably.

Only one incident occurred that is worthy to be related. One morning Val Prinsep—who lived next door to Leighton, and who, as well as being a painter, was the husband of the daughter of Leland, for whom Whistler painted the celebrated Peacock Room, and of whom he also painted, and in his best manner, a large caricature, as a cloven-footed and horned devil, sitting strumming on a piano, with large purses on the floor and piano, inscribed "filthy lucre," which picture now hangs in the drawing-room of Mrs. Spreckles, of San Francisco—came in to breakfast, and a talk began between him and Leighton upon some of the painters of the day. They agreed with Ruskin's criticisms, or rather abuse, of Whistler's work, and thought he was amply rewarded in the libel suit by a farthing. There might be some merit in his etchings, and a little to like in the Valparaiso Bay, but as for the Connie Gilchrist, with the skipping-rope, that was an unforgivable impertinence.

But when they came to Sargent, I pricked up my ears and listened, to my utter bewilderment, to such a tirade of abuse of that unfortunate man's style, that I began at last to offer a protest, and to defend critically an Art which then seemed to outshine in brilliancy and in dashing technique the work of any other. It then transpired that Lord Leighton agreed with Prinsep about Sargent, and predicted for him, as well as for all the modern French school, beginning with Manet and ending with Monet, a well-merited oblivion within a few years. "These fellows think I do not understand them, that I am not in the movement, and never can be," said Leighton. "That is not the case. I understand perfectly what they are driving at, but this thing is not for me; I simply do not like it. As for Sargent, he will go no further. They talk of electing him to the Academy, but that will never be." "Never," chimed in Prinsep, with determination and will, as he drew himself up in his chair, and planted his two doubled-up fists down on the table.

"Don't you think they will have to elect him some day? Most of the young men admire him, and even one of the older members of the Academy," I ventured rather timidly. "No! no! Not at all. We do not want him; his influence is bad. Look at his drawing, his colour! The long, skinny arms and fantastic, pink fingers are enough to frighten any woman away from his studio—and his great brush-sweeps, mere daubs without meaning." "But," I murmured, when the chance permitted, in a lull, "you might have said the same of Sir Joshua, of Raeburn, and, more particularly, of Romney. Are not Romney's portraits as freely painted, without Sargent's accuracy of drawing? "Pooh! pooh! mere chance and guesswork. He relies upon accidental tints and colours and blendings to produce an effect, without any solid basis of drawing, or painstaking execution." And so they continued without a single word of praise for work which had already been acclaimed in Paris, and was attracting in the more conservative quarters of London an attention that was soon to develop into admiration, and ultimately to create a school of portraiture that became universal.

These two men were both sincere. Apart from that spontaneous and irresistible jealousy and chagrin that men of established position often feel at the too sudden flaring up of youthful genius which casts a shadow upon them, and tends to relegate them to comparative obscurity, there could have been no motive underlying this frank expression of feeling. Did they think that the prestige of English Art was endangered?

In Lord Leighton the Academy lost a great president. He lived and worked in the last days of traditions and conservatism. His contemporaries were Gladstone, Beaconsfield, Salisbury, and Chamberlain—the men who framed the Constitution of England on purely Conservative lines. Since their time chaos has reigned in Art as in politics.

GEORGE MEREDITH

THERE is a pretty old inn at Burford Bridge where, I believe, Keats wrote the line, "A thing of beauty is a joy for ever," and calling it out of the window to his friend Leigh Hunt, who was lying on the grass in the sun, Hunt called back, "That will live for ever."

Poor Keats! Poor Poe! With what riches they endowed a thoughtless and ungrateful world! Can it be much of a consolation to their spirits to know that a wealth of sentiment is now showered upon the tombs that hold their once hungering and starved bodies? What law of chance governs rewards and punishments? Who can explain the affluence of a Peter Paul Rubens, a Velasquez, or a Benjamin West, and the poverty of a Rembrandt, a Franz Hals, and a Gilbert Stuart? An Alma Tadema may live in a palace with a golden stair, while a Mathew Maris shades the smoking oil-lamp, that lights his humble room, with a newspaper.

Not far from the inn on the side of Box Hill the author of The Egoist lived—lived and suffered, though he did not die young—in a small Georgian house of ugly, commonplace design, approached through a flowerless front garden hemmed in on all sides by a great box hedge that frowned gloomily down upon bewildered visitors.

It would be idle to attempt to demonstrate that passions are allayed by beautiful surroundings; for crime is as

prevalent in the palace as in the hut; but as romancers, especially French writers, frequently lay the scene of a tragedy in an isolated and forsaken-looking dwelling of forbidding aspect, so the close student of the psychology of the passionate or criminal mind may find his reveries disturbed by the contemplation of flowering honeysuckle, or rose, or sweet-scented lavender, or any innocent and beautiful fact of Nature that steals upon the inner contemplation of a direful plot based upon human misery.

Sin may be simple and sweet and forgivable, or it may be bitter and remorseful; and when the theme is of the latter kind, the romancer is no Oliver Goldsmith, singing of lowing kine and daisy-besprinkled meadows, but a Hardy or a Meredith devoted to introspection and the causes of human imperfections. Do such men love beauty, or even know it when they see it? Beauty is superficial: a sentiment lies beneath the surface, has to be searched for, is pricked into being. An analysis of the sentiment aroused by the emotion of beauty is a very different thing from the simple contemplation of beauty.

That George Meredith was filled with the emotion of beauty is manifest in his prose and his verse. Love of colour, form, harmony and contrast; a knowledge of Nature and Nature's art speak everywhere in his books. Sunrise and sunset thrilled him through and through, and he gave joyous utterance to a flood of words descriptive of the moving images that the ever-changing cloud-forms suggested to his imagination.

Yet we expect some expression of the artist's inner life in his home or his workshop; and that Swinburne, the sensuous singer of amatory graces, should have lived in a mean, bourgeois, terraced house in Putney, with his watch-dog, Watts Dunton, is much more incomprehensible than that Meredith, who held the palm among contemporary English prose writers, should have hidden himself in a prosaic cottage at Box Hill.

Yet Burford Bridge has its associations; and here I was sent, by my friend Mr. Edward H. Coates, to paint a portrait of the novelist most beloved by the cognoscenti of America, for the portrait gallery of the Pennsylvania Academy. "We must have Meredith," wrote Mr. Coates, "for we all love his books."

Meredith was recovering from the shock of a fall that had broken his ankle, and I found him resting his foot upon a chair as he half reclined in another. He was not happy in his mind. The long convalescence and confinement in the house vexed him; the social conditions of the day—what would he have thought of this day?—the gross inequalities in the distribution of wealth, the growing unrest of the people, weighed upon him. He wrote letters to the newspapers about it all, but he offered no remedy. He talked about America, about Philadelphia, and recalled Weir Mitchell and his books. And as he talked, I studied him, his colour, his expression, and his general characteristics.

The inn where I stayed was bright and sunny, and the rooms very comfortable; so I lingered long to see more of the recluse, for so he seemed, shut in, as it were, behind the hedges that hid him from the road and the passing people—like Tennyson, in his later life, concealed from view in his hidden gardens at Freshwater. Meredith followed the example of other great thinkers who become shy in their old age and withdraw from the world. There are men who resent the change from strength to weakness, from the ruddy glow of health in firm and solid cheeks to the pallor and the wan, frail look of decaying faculties. Swinburne put the matter tersely by saying he was not young enough to be beautiful and not old enough to be picturesque, when he refused to sit for his portrait. So few know when the picturesqueness begins, and sometimes it never comes at all—it is frequently a question of hair!

At last I obtained material enough to make the portrait, and the work was accomplished to the satisfaction of the President of the Pennsylvania Academy of the Fine Arts, and now hangs in the Historic Portrait Collection of that institution.

ALFRED GILBERT

ALFRED GILBERT is the modern Cellini and the greatest of all English sculptors. He has more originality than Alfred Stevens, and surpasses him beyond measure in knowledge and technical skill—in this last he is unrivalled. Cellini has given us the Perseus and a number of small pieces; Gilbert has enriched the field of English sculpture with many noble monuments and a series of decorative pieces that surpass in design and execution the best of Cellini's table ornaments.

When Gilbert was working upon the Lord Mayor's chain, I asked him if he did not fear that the jeweller's art, that then seemed to fascinate him, would interfere with his hand and eye, and tend to diminish the loftiness of his conception of great monuments. His reply was that the study of small things would enlarge his vision and improve his technical ability to deal with big work.

He was at this time engaged upon the construction of the fountain that now stands in Piccadilly Circus. As I looked at this work, looming large in the confined space of the studio, I felt instinctively that when erected in the open it would so diminish in appearance as to be dwarfed by the surrounding buildings. He did not agree with me, and explained that it was sometimes moved out into the street, behind the studio, in order that its scale might be accurately gauged. The street was smaller than the studio, making the test useless. His attention was being expended upon the helmeted boy holding the gurnet. The details of the head and fins of the fish were to him some of Nature's jewellery, and on these he devoted his love of subtle mimicry. Fishes and fins, fresh and stale, wet and dry, littered the tables and stands around him. Cherubs in helmets, holding real and plaster gurnets in every conceivable position, were poised upon the fountain. On this his genius was not thrown away, for the helmeted boy and his fish, repeated at every corner of the base of what is sometimes ironically called the "pulpit," form the masterpiece of the fountain. My anticipation that the mass of the fountain would be on too small a scale for its situation was realized. A work that would have graced a terrace in a nobleman's garden is out of place in Piccadilly.

The tomb of King George's brother, the Duke of Clarence, in Windsor Chapel, is, perhaps, a justification of Gilbert's contention that the study of detail in precious ornamentation may be an aid to the sculptor; for in this superb work the master has lavished all his affection upon the figures in armour that stand as guardians to the dead Prince within the catafalque. Here the scale is proportioned to the site.

In the memorial to Queen Victoria, Gilbert's sense of decoration, as well as of proportion, enabled him to disguise, by a masterly arrangement of the draperies of the royal robes, the short and corpulent figure of the sovereign, and to present Her Majesty in a manner fitting the dignity of the wearer of the crown of the Empire. Here realism is not outraged or disregarded, it is merely embellished by things as real as the Queen herself, and which add to the beauty of the monument.

No one but Rodin could have presented a naked Victor Hugo without shocking us; but genius will accomplish miracles of audacity where talent does not dare to go beyond a conventional formula.

One of Gilbert's early works, The Sleeper, I am told, is destroyed. Those who remember the figure of the young girl, relaxed in slumber, and almost sinking into the great arm-chair under the spell of the bird that broods over her unconscious form, will be glad to have been privileged to see one of the glories of English art before it disappeared for ever.

Gilbert is a stoutly built, powerful man with a strong, square head and masterful jaw. There is in type a striking resemblance to Beethoven; and this resemblance finds justification in the musical ability of the sculptor, inherited from his musician father.

It is enough now to touch lightly upon the artist's work; to treat of the man would be beyond the knowledge and power of any one writer. Those who knew him intimately are dead. Like Cellini, he alone is capable of revealing the vicissitudes of a career that would have surpassed the Italian master's amazing life, had the modern English genius lived in the sixteenth century.

ONSLOW FORD

WHO can describe this gentle and amiable man? With the allure of the garçon du Quartier Latin, although I believe he studied only for a short time in Paris, his inner personality was that of a true-born, loyal Briton, with that intense love of home and of family life which is characteristic of the race. He was all his life dominated by two strong affections—love of his family and love of Art; and, as is usual where a man is not single-hearted in his loves, jealousies and conflicts occurred between the rival passions. But he was strong and patient in the depths of a nature that on the surface was so frail and fragile, that it vibrated like the leaves of an aspen at each breath of wind or touch of sunshine.

He was born to enjoy much, and to suffer much. His life was comparable to the ever-restless seas that pass from buoyancy to calm, and from calm to storm, under the changing moods of mobile skies. We met in early life, and we walked side by side in joy and in sorrow until he died, nearly twenty years ago. He moulded his Follies and his Singers, "little waxen figures," as a "friendly critic" once called them, and I limned my little portraits of big men; and we both were happy at our work and in our homes.

We mingled in the throngs of men in Piccadilly or on the Boulevards like two exotics, our pointed beards and long moustaches ébouriffées, hats with straight brims, à la Whistler, pegtop trousers, and square-toed low shoes, with silken ties making us more at home sur les Boulevards than in Piccadilly. I was the first to degenerate into the normal style, but Ford hung on to the flowing tie until the last, and in the height of his success he had his imitators. I shall never forget the effect he produced in Chatham, at the time of the unveiling of his statue to Gordon, as he walked alone down the main street, upon the provincial populace of that truly British town, who greeted him with shouts of "Frenchy!" quite unconscious of the fact that they were acclaiming the hero of the hour.

Onslow Ford, as I have said, was in no sense a Frenchman, either in blood, in habits, or in education. He studied in Munich, the most artistic of all the towns of Germany, where he at first made so little progress in drawing and painting that one of his heartless teachers told him to return to his home and take up shoemaking. He followed his advice in part, gave up drawing and painting, and entered the studio of a sculptor. Here he found the bent of his mind, and followed it with success, which proves that talent must be trained in the direction of its growth, and not against it.

It was not long before his work began to attract the attention it deserved. The Royal Academy welcomed him as a member, and one important commission after another followed in close succession. But it is not so much as an artist that I wish to consider him, but as a man. His Shelley, at Oxford, is a beautiful and pathetic figure, but the two works that I love are Folly, the first of the small bronzes, and the last marble, A Snowflake. The latter, a frail young girl, seems to be melting out of life, just as the creator himself melted slowly away. It was his last work. How typical are these two statues of his nature and his life! He admired frost and dreaded it. To him heat was life, and cold death.

He both gave and received friendship. His was that rare and perfect amity that anticipated desire and hastened to gratify it almost before the friend was conscious of a want. It was l'âme that spoke from the inner consciousness of a dependent nature, the only lovable nature.

He was intensely religious. He worshipped the emotions of beauty, love, charity, fidelity, loyalty. One incident in his life will reveal the tenderness and gentleness of his disposition. A celebrated athlete, named Jones, a runner who had outstripped Lightfoot, the Indian, had been converted at a Moody and Sankey meeting, and gave up the ring to be an evangelist. Finding that this did not enable him to provide for his wife and family, he became a model. Having overstrained his lungs in running, he developed consumption and wasted slowly over a period of years. During this time Ford and I employed him to sit for us, and as we permitted Jones to talk upon his religious experiences, the former pugilist conceived a great liking for both of us. Once on returning from a journey I was hurriedly visited by Ford, who begged me to go with him at once to see the dying Jones, whom he had been caring for and comforting in my absence.

When we entered his room we found the poor man, a living skeleton, lying on his back, breathing his last. Only his eyes seemed to be alive, and on seeing us they filled with a joyful light that seemed to illumine supernaturally his shrunken and pallid face. Seating ourselves one on each side of him and taking his waxlike hands, we bent down to hear his last few words of adieu, of faith and hope. While he was speaking, the notes of the hymn "Nearer, my God, to Thee" were wafted from the street below through the open windows. Turning suddenly upon his side, he breathed a long and contented sigh, and died.

HENRY THOURON

SOON after the end of the Civil War in America my father sent me to the art school of George Holmes, in Philadelphia, where I met Henry Thouron. He was about two years my senior. He called me John, and placed his arm over my shoulder, half in affection and half, so it seemed to me, in protection. His strong arm, the symbol of his spiritual strength, has ever since been on my shoulder, and is still there, although he died in Rome four years ago.

My recollection of the work we did under the tuition of Mr. Holmes is very imperfect, but I suppose it consisted in imitating, in crayons, the lithographed drawings of casts from Greek and Roman busts and statues, a very roundabout way to arrive at proficiency in drawing, or in any sort of accuracy of observation. All the budding artists of Pennsylvania met in the studio of Mr. Holmes. From there they drifted to the schools of the Pennsylvania Academy of the Fine Arts, then located in Chestnut Street, under the presidency of Richard Vaux, who, many years afterwards, while I was painting him, asked me why people were making so much fuss about Art then, because in the old days, when he was President of the Academy, no one ever gave it a thought, or even came to see the pictures.

About this time the Academy building was turned into a theatre. Benjamin West's great pictures of Death on the Pale Horse and Christ before Pilate and others were stored out of sight, and the plaster casts and the students removed to temporary quarters in various parts of the city, until the projected new Academy could be built on Broad Street, from the designs of Frank Furness.

Thouron and I moved with the casts, and placed ourselves under the guidance of Professor Schüssele, from Düsseldorf. It was here that Edwin Abbey pursued his studies, and I can remember a charcoal drawing, of

Hamlet soliloquizing, that he submitted to the professor of composition. Henry Thouron gave his attention from the beginning to composition. The grouping of figures in masses and their relation to the surrounding architecture or landscape inspired him from the start, and after a long career as professor of composition, at the Academy, he finished it in Rome, by executing the second of two large decorative panels which he designed for the cathedral in Logan Square.

In Philadelphia we were in constant companionship, and I could not have failed to benefit by the example of a conduct so straightforward, so disinterested, and so ingenuous, or from the observation of a mind whose charity and goodwill were surpassed only by its purity and nobility.

In Europe we drifted apart, Thouron having selected Bonnat's studio, in Paris, as his workshop, while I, by adventure, or misadventure perhaps, wandered to the Flemish Academy of Antwerp. But we were in constant correspondence, and for a short period found ourselves again associated in Paris.

It was here that I was able to consider more closely the restraining influence of religious faith upon a nature that was in its undertones both ardent and passionate. To live in amity among the libres penseurs and the libertines who composed the classes of the atelier Bonnat proved the American student to be not only a man of the most virile character, but one who followed the Lord in the prayer, "Father forgive them; they know not what they do." I have had occasion myself to rebuke one of his classmates for ridiculing him at table on account of his faithful observance of a religious ceremony that has now almost entirely fallen into desuetude among all sects.

From Paris Thouron passed on through Italy to Rome, and there continued his studies for a number of years. It was here that he met with young Alfred Gilbert, that English genius whom England had not the patience to conquer, or the wit to understand. Gilbert was then casting, by the cire perdu process, his bronze figure of Icarus which now stands in the hall of Leighton House, a tribute to the discerning patronage of Lord Leighton, who was President of the Royal Academy when the modern Cellini arrived from Rome to astound the people of London by the fertility of his imagination and the dexterity of his execution. To such a man the presence of a kindly counsellor like Thouron might have meant salvation.

It is almost impossible to describe Henry Thouron. I knew him as intimately as he permitted anyone to know him, save his mother and his sister, to whom he was passionately devoted, and always closely associated. His nature was both simple and complex. His supersensitive and over-scrupulous temperament dictated actions that were frequently misunderstood. Men who pride themselves upon being men of the world live often in conventional and narrow limits beyond which, or above which, their savoir faire does not permit them to see. To such men Henry Thouron was an enigma. "We know," say they, "the altar and the hearth, the forum and the market-place. What lies beyond?" That which lies beyond they do not know, and it was in "the beyond" that Henry Thouron lived, thought, and worked.

Ruskin has said, in one of his lectures, that classicalism began wherever civilization began, with Pagan faith; mediævalism began and continued wherever civilization began, and continued, to confess Christ; and, lastly, modernism began and continues wherever civilization began, and continues, to deny Christ. Since Ruskin delivered this lecture, in Edinburgh in the year 1853, the denials of Christ are growing louder and louder, and the cocks are crowing lustily.

Ruskin has given away Thouron's secret—he was a mediævalist; he was born four centuries too late. He should have been a contemporary of Raphael. The dress of Giotto would have suited him. It was often my privilege to be admitted to his studio when he was working on the large decoration for the cathedral. Standing high on the scaffolding, with a gray linen blouse pulled over his modern clothes, he was transformed into a fresco painter of the fifteenth century. In physique, in bearing, in colour, and in physiognomy he was mediæval—his spirit haunted the aisles of the Gothic cathedrals. His sole ambition seemed to inspire him to make his own church, to confess Christ on every wall and in every aisle.

To this end he became a patron of Art as well as an artist, showing even here the religious spirit of the princes of the Church and the State, who, in those times, made it possible for the genius of a Michael Angelo or a Giotto to develop and flourish. Henry Thouron knew, as Ruskin knew, that "all ancient Art was religious and all modern art is profane," and he therefore worked zealously to restore Art to its sacred function. He stood among the few in his city as a generous and unselfish patron of Art, and he proved that patronage is not the privilege of the rich only, but of all who love beauty, and cultivate a taste for it; that men of modest means may possess gems of modern Art by ever-increasing care and discrimination in selecting them.

He devoted many years to the teaching of composition in the classrooms of the Pennsylvania Academy, where he came into close and friendly relations with all the students, from whom he received to the last the warmest tokens of regard and esteem, and from his colleagues a silent admiration evoked by the invariable gentleness of his disposition.

To me he was particularly sympathetic; and I remember how long I lingered over the little portrait painted in his studio, solely to enjoy the repose of mind his companionship gave me.

After he died, Harrison S. Morris, who, as managing director of the Academy, had been associated with him and his work, wrote:

"He gave so abundantly of all he had—his means, his strength—that I always felt about him as the friends of Saint Francis of Assisi spoke of their saint. He had realized sainthood in a time when even Saint Francis might have been appalled at the lack of beauty and sincerity, and at the noise and shock of life. He was an artist of the beautiful, if ever there was one. His taste was like the taste of Nature that never errs when not thwarted by man.... Indeed, his life was one long devotion, either to his faith, in which the old beauty appealed deeply to him, or to the service of those to whom he could, with his abundant talents, minister. I think he felt that a mediæval world of simple faith and the haunting mystery of loveliness was his real habitation, but that accident had translated him to our ugly and brazen days. "Hardly in even many more lifetimes will so pure and clean a spirit visit the earth."

RICHARD VAUX

WALKING with my son, in Chestnut Street, Philadelphia, one day long ago, when the boy's curls were still hanging over his small shoulders, I said to him, "Do you see that tall old man over there with long hair like yours? That is Mr. Richard Vaux, Mayor of Philadelphia. Go over and speak to him, and tell him that your father has sent you to greet him with the message that he will be at his office at eleven o'clock for a sitting for the portrait. He will understand. I want to see you standing together."

And a remarkable sight it was to see the tall and erect figure of Richard Vaux, one of the great characters of the city, bend over to the little boy with golden curls and take his hand. The flowing, ash-coloured hair of the Mayor had a crinkle in it that held it out, fan-like, beneath a broad-brimmed silk hat, whose crown was much too tall and elegant to be the hat of a Quaker. The tight-fitting, closely buttoned frock-coat, with ample skirt that hung shapely over trousers that wrinkled upon the instep of polished low shoes, tied with bows, made up a personality that had no counterpart in that or any other city. The Gladstone collar should not be forgotten, although to call Richard Vaux's collar a Gladstone was post-dating a style—a sort of atrophy of the old stock—used in America when Gladstone was an Oxford undergraduate. The background to these two strongly contrasted, and yet characteristically similar, figures was the display of roses and lilies in the window of Pennock's flower shop; and the peculiar picturesqueness of the scene began soon to attract the attention of passers-by, from whose curiosity and admiration I had to rescue them by taking the boy away.

At eleven o'clock I was admitted to the law offices of the distinguished old Quaker, where a portrait, already half finished, was waiting on the easel for the morning's work. The room was indescribable. A faint notion of its character can be obtained from the portrait, in which the accessories are rendered as faithfully in regard to condition and disposition as could be; for Mr. Vaux did not limit me either in the number or extent of the sittings, and I prolonged them purposely, in order to obtain as much of the detail as possible, and also for the pleasure he always gave me by talking, more or less at random, upon politics, signs of the times, philosophy, and religion. One of his favourite and persistent ejaculations was, "I can hear the ringing of the spurs and the clanking of the sword of the man on horseback." As the Republican Party was always in power in Pennsylvania, he had come to the conclusion that a military dictatorship would be necessary to dislodge it. Between puffs at his cigar—there is one lighted and smoking on the table in the portrait—he would vent his views on the iniquities of all sorts perpetrated by the administrators of the city. He liked the sittings, because he found in me a sympathetic listener. The room was hazy with smoke, through which its unusual picturesqueness appealed to me as no other lawyer's office could do. Those that I have seen in America have been too spick and span, too well ordered, and the books too obviously new, in conventional yellow calf or sheep-skin, with bright red labels.

These were all faded, musty tomes, beautified by age and dust and repose—for Mr. Vaux had given up the practice of the law—and they were so numerous that the shelves and chairs and floors were encumbered by them. Here and there packages of bright blue and green pamphlets, lying loosely about and under the tables, gave a little colour to a scene of soft browns and smoky grays.

In downright picturesqueness, Richard Vaux, in his study, surpassed Mr. Gladstone in the Temple of Peace. And it was not premeditated, for although Mr. Vaux had been President of the Pennsylvania Academy of the Fine Arts, when the Academy building was in Chestnut Street, his artistic impulses were not strong, and he startled me one morning by asking abruptly, "What is the meaning of all this present-day Art talk? When I was President of the Academy no one ever gave Art a thought, and the picture galleries were always empty."

Richard Vaux was a democrat of the old school, which meant, in the Southern States, an aristocrat—an inconsistency in party names as curious as party shibboleths. He believed in tariffs for revenue only, and abhorred protection. His father had extracted from him a promise in his youth that he would never enter a theatre; and although he must have been often tempted to join theatre parties while he was attaché to the American legation in London, he never broke the promise. He was over eighty years of age when I painted him.

When speaking of religion he broke into the discussion by thumping his hand down upon a book, exclaiming, "I believe this book from cover to cover." It was the Bible.

EDWARD MANDELL HOUSE

IN the summer of 1919, a few weeks before leaving America, I made a hasty trip to Oyster Bay, the once favourite residence of Colonel Roosevelt, to select among the names of a number of men who had become prominent during the war one whom I would be willing to paint for a national portrait gallery.

Several names were mentioned, but when that of "Colonel" House came up, I said, "That will do; I would rather paint him than any man in the country, not excepting the President." As the Colonel was then in Europe, as envoy plenipotentiary to the Peace Congress, and as I expected to be in London and Paris within a few weeks, a letter was sent to him asking him to grant me sittings.

I had not been in London more than three days before a cable message from New York arrived telling me to go to Paris at once, where the sittings had been arranged. Before leaving London a lady, who seemed to know Colonel House, told me I should not like him. For some reason, known only to herself, she made a statement which in the sequel proved to be peculiarly misjudged, for I have rarely met anyone I have liked more.

I must confess that one of my reasons for selecting Colonel House to paint was due to a feeling of curiosity to know him, and, if possible, to discover the secret of his apparent power over President Wilson.

Colonel House was living at the Hôtel Crillon, facing the Place de la Concorde, where many of the American missions were established, with their staffs. The Colonel received me with unusual grace and simplicity of manner, and in a voice of peculiar personal charm assured me of his goodwill towards the project in view. His friendliness was like that of one who had known me for years; all restraint was at once broken down, and although I recognized in him an unlimited reserve of both firmness and sternness, his chief apparent characteristic was an easy naturalness, blended with a manly gentleness, that might have deceived the unwary.

After making two slight sketches in charcoal, I began to paint. When the portrait was partially finished, the light seemed too dull to complete it; so the position was changed to one near the window, where a strong light was reflected from a wall opposite. Choosing the position of reading a book, the head slightly turned down, I painted the eyes raised and looking straight at me.

Colonel House's eyes are remarkable. Looking at him casually, an ordinary observer might see nothing uncommon in their general character or expression; but the quiet intensity of their gaze opens mysterious depths of latent feeling. That Colonel House knew their power is told in the following story: When Lloyd George first called to see him, Colonel House asked him to take a seat with his back to the window and his face in shadow, while the Colonel seated himself in full light opposite the window. As Lloyd George expressed some surprise at this, saying that the usual practice was to put the visitor in the light, where his emotions could be more easily read, Colonel House replied, "I do not need to see my visitors; I want them to see me, as I might have reason for downing them."

When Mrs. House came in one morning to see the portrait, she exclaimed at once, "I do not like it. I have never seen that look on his face." Turning to her, I said apologetically, "I am not painting a husband, but a public man." This did not convince her, although the secretary said afterwards to Colonel House that she knew the look very well and liked it. As no objection was made, I brought another canvas and painted the "husband," with his hat on, which pleased the wife and every one.

Colonel House is a small man, but he told me that he was the tallest of the five heads of the council who met at his house to discuss quietly the subjects of the day before going to Versailles. Here, in a room gaily decorated in bright, flowered damask, sat around a table five small men, representing the combined victorious military and naval power of the world—Clemenceau, Lloyd George, Colonel House, Orlando, and, the smallest of all, but by no means the least, Maréchal Foch.

The description of these gatherings stirred the imagination. In my mind's eye the five small men, the modern Cæsars and Napoleons, rose before me, all save one, the Napoleon of the company, dressed unbecomingly in tweeds and serges that assorted ill with the brocaded chairs—the wise old French statesman, the shrewd Briton, the suave Italian, the sphinx-like American, and the straight-forward soldier. Here was the historic subject of the war. Colonel House realized it even more vividly than I, and temptingly suggested the possibility of obtaining sittings for it. But I heard afterwards that the room had been dismantled by a modiste. A background could have been faked up; but when I thought how each one of these heroes had been beset by interviewers, photographers, and painters and sculptors, in addition perhaps to scissor artists, I concluded that I would not inspire in them a further hatred for the processes of Art.

Colonel House revealed only two things to me—his amiability and his idealism. Almost he persuaded me, by the former quality, to embrace the latter. When he said good-bye, a day or two before he sailed for America, my sympathy for him had been so strongly aroused that I was betrayed, by an emotion that it was impossible to suppress, to wish him success in the high aim which he shared with President Wilson, although my reason forbade me to harbour an illusion which in my heart of hearts I thoroughly disliked. If the races were ready for a universal dominion, there would be no need for it.

COSMO MONKHOUSE

THE last time I saw Cosmo Monkhouse was in the garden of George F. Watts, in Melbury Road. "Signor" was entertaining, and as I descended the steps, leading from the studio to the garden, the first person I met was Monkhouse, who greeted me with, "Isidora Duncan is dancing my poems!" The dear old man was brimful of joy and merriment, because the graceful American was following the measure and rhythm of his verse in harmonious movements of the body, as they were read slowly, in musical cadences.

Isidora's languorous undulations among the rhododendrons and under the deep purple clematis that hung in flowering festoons above her, against a background formed of the eager faces of the gaily dressed guests, made a picture to thrill a poet; and the sensitive eye of Monkhouse gathered in the vision with the greater emotion because he felt that he had inspired it.

"Signor" stood watching, his fine profile, white beard, and half-mediæval dress adding to the quaint and unusual picture a note in form and colour that raised the scene far above the conventional level of a full-dress garden party. I had seen Isidora dance years before, and I have seen her since, imitating the movements of the Greek dance as depicted on the old vases; but the pleasure I received in Watts's garden was enhanced by the frankly expressed new joy of my old friend, whose song was being danced as well as sung.

I enjoyed painting Monkhouse, because he was a good sitter, a good and sympathetic talker, and he had an interesting head. And I am glad I painted him, because this tale can be told.

The portrait was done, years before the above garden scene occurred, in the oak-panelled room at Murestead, where I also painted William Richards, the American sea painter, Croal Thomson, and where I should have painted

Phil May, as he came in one day, all booted and spurred from a ride in the park. A little incident in connection with this portrait is worth telling. At a crowded entertainment, where Onslow Ford and I were jammed in among a number of Academicians, Herkomer squeezed through the crowd to where we were standing and said to me, "I like so much your little portrait of Monkhouse; I will give it a good place," and then passed on.

When he was out of hearing, Ford said, "He should not have told you that; it is contrary to the etiquette and rule of the Academy. Just imagine what you would think, if your portrait did not get a good place, or even was not hung." I had not been surprised by Herkomer's frank praise and promise; but I was very much surprised and even hurt by Ford's attitude and his censure of Herkomer. I would not have missed the open compliment for all the secret etiquette in the world. And Herkomer was quite sure of himself and true to his word; for the Monkhouse was given a centre in the gallery allotted to small canvases.

But it is painful to have to tell that some years after this a similar thing happened, and I had to suffer the consequences that Ford had prevised. I had sent in the last portrait I had made of Mr. Gladstone. Some time before the opening of the Academy, Edwin Abbey said, "I like your portrait of Gladstone, and will get it a good place." It was hung high against the jamb of a door, where it could not be seen!

HENRI ROCHEFORT

WHILE I was painting Henri Rochefort, in Paris, I called to see my former master, Gérome. He was old and gray, and tired. He had worked too hard, and yet he was still hard at it, finishing a bronze statue of young Napoleon on horseback, a Tamerlane, his horse bestriding un monceau de têtes de mort, and painting at two or three canvases on the easels. After a little talk about himself and his work, he asked me what I was doing. "A portrait of Rochefort," was my answer. "Rochefort!" he exclaimed, in a strident voice, "Ne pourriez vous pas trouver autre chose à faire que cela? Rochefort! Cet homme-là a fait plus de mal à la France que n'importe quel autre de nos jours. C'est un miserable!" Et il poursuivit d'injures l'editeur de l'Intransigeant. Je me tus, je ne savais que répondre. Enfin j'osais balbutier, "Mais, il est si pittoresque, il a une chevelure." Gérome était tellement courroucé que je trouvais bon de m'esquiver.

Henri Rochefort was the man of the chevelure à la cockatoo, of whom a colossal bust was made by Rodin, in his most brutal manner. He was for many years a well-known figure in London, a political exile. One remarked him in Piccadilly, in the same way as one noticed Sir Squire Bancroft with his head in the air seeming to overlook everybody through his monocle. How very few remarkable figures there are, figures that stand out conspicuously among a mass of mediocrities!

Rochefort could have been seen, with his handsome niece, constantly in Christie's auction rooms, watching the sales of pictures and furniture. After his return to Paris I commenced the portrait at his house. It was never finished. The Dreyfus affair was at its hottest. At first I was not interested, but a New York lady, who lived always in Europe, called my attention to the apparent injustice of the officer's conviction, degradation, and exile. After reading Zola's famous letter, J'accuse, I became a Dreyfusard, and followed every aspect of le petit bleu with ardour and excitement.

It was an unfortunate moment to be closeted with Henri Rochefort. The French language contained no epithet strong enough, no cochonnerie vile enough to convey Rochefort's spleen against this unfortunate "spy," who was not only in league with the Devil, but, what was far worse, with the Emperor William of Germany. There was no doubt at all in Rochefort's mind that the Emperor himself was in constant secret communication with Dreyfus, and that the fireproof safe, in his palace at Potsdam, contained documents supplied by his correspondent in France, revealing the strength and the weakness of the French army, the characters of the personnel of the staff, the number and calibre of the guns, and the definitions of all the secret mechanisms and appliances of the various armaments.

Rochefort did not believe in original sin, and vigorously pooh-poohed the idea that little children, pure and innocent angels, as he called them, could possibly be inheritors of the germs of wickedness. But original sin and all other kinds of sin were innate in the Kaiser and in the traitorous miscreant who had betrayed France to the grasp of the "mailed fist," the foe acharné de la Patrie.

Whatever may have been the views of English statesmen in 1896, Henri Rochefort harboured no illusions as to the ambitions and aims of the German Emperor.

In the light of what has transpired since, a light that blazed red for four years, I may have done Rochefort an injustice by quitting his house before the portrait was finished, because of the vehemence of his invective against the enemies of France and the unfortunate Dreyfus.

GENERAL BOOTH

THE most benevolent figure in England in the nineteenth century, perhaps the greatest personality in the world, is that of the organizer and the leader of the Salvation Army.

If we look back over a hundred years, the really conspicuous names are few in number—Napoleon, Wellington, Washington, Lincoln, Gladstone, Disraeli, and Bismarck. Of these seven, one, Lincoln, stood for a sentiment—not a principle. He fought for what is called freedom, whereas the great principle in nature is dependence, and its first duty is service. Not every one in his country agreed with him, for one-third of its population attacked him for his interference with their right to govern themselves and maintain their own institutions. And in the end, a brother of the celebrated actor Booth slew him, and shouting to the stupefied audience in the theatre "Sic semper tyrannis," fled from the scene.

Was Lincoln right or was he wrong? This is a question that will be answered, as nature generally answers, by an enigmatic casting of events, before the end of this century.

Reading history from the historian's standpoint is misleading and confusing; but reading it from the impeccable evidence impressed upon stones, and from the works of the men of the different epochs themselves, we can arrive more closely at the truth. Quoting only one historian, who will serve as an example for the others, Guizot, in his History of Civilization, says: "In this century (the fourteenth) painting in oils was discovered." How illuminating is such a statement upon the condition of Art in Europe! In the whole book no other comment is made upon Art, as though it were merely a decorative fringe on a garment woven, not in cloth of gold and silver, but of mail, hammered out by the forgerons of war. Ignoring completely the fact that Art, and Art only, made civilization possible, he talks profusely and learnedly of the conflicts between the sovereigns of the Church and the State, and of the rivalries between barons and kings.

Now what do the stones teach? They show us that in Greece and Rome civilization reached its highest expression in temple and in statue, and in all the arts of the hearth and home, as well as of the altar. And what historian has described the literature of the time and the thought and customs of the people so well as the makers of the literature themselves?

The inference is, then, that the Greeks and the Romans, because of the principle of slavery, of enforced service, or whatever one chooses to call it, possessed that undisturbed leisure which is necessary to the growth and the development of intellectual powers. Society was clearly divided into two classes—the servers and the served. Without doubt the slaves formed the more numerous class, and they comprised all grades, all colours, and all nationalities. They were both skilled and learned, and often attained to high offices of responsibility, under owners who were merely nominal masters.

The men of leisure, the intellectuals, and the artists were not concerned about that part of the machinery of life which fed, bathed, and clothed the community. Life was infinitely easier, because it was conducted upon military principles of order and obedience. Art, literature, games and spectacles flourished, as they have never flourished since, and even war was conducted with an ease and efficiency that laughs the moderns to scorn.

It is supposed to have been a great feat on the part of Napoleon that he crossed the Alps. Julius Cæsar crossed them many times and encompassed territories that Napoleon was never able to reach with all his modern appliances, and with the aid of skilful generals.

If slavery helped pagan civilization to rise, the principles of Christianity were probably the main causes of its decline—they certainly undermined the Roman Empire. No such doctrine as "He who lives by the sword shall perish by the sword" could permeate the minds of the Romans without weakening their military spirit; and the converse will be the case in our own time, for the British Empire will fall when the principles of Christianity are ignored or forgotten, and the white peoples will fall with it. Dominion is not a question of whiteness or blackness; it is a question of capacity and faith. It has been necessary to make the above points clear in order to understand the position of General Booth in his generation.

In the first place his work has succeeded, and he lived to see its success. In a different manner Napoleon, Wellington, and Washington were successful. Napoleon placed France in the forefront of the nations, and established the foundations of a future eminence that had been shattered by the Revolution; Wellington and Nelson—for the two cannot be separated—guarded England against Napoleon's vaulting ambition and opened the vista of an Empire of freedom and justice; Washington founded a state which is now destined to see the last of our modern civilization. General Booth created an ecclesiastical authority of which he was the great high-priest. There was a universal need for such a man; and the man was forthcoming. The churches had ceased to perform efficiently their functions towards that part of the community most in want of their succour and support. They continued to ring carillons, to toll vespers, and to say "Come"; but Booth went to those who no longer had ears to hear, or minds to obey. He sought them out in their lairs, and, having first cleansed their bodies, he spoke the divine message of love to their hearts, baptizing them with water, and then, through the spoken word, with the Spirit of God.

"But other men have done the like," you say. That is true; but have they done as much as General Booth? He was no gentle Christian, tender of touch, and soft of speech, satisfied with winning a soul here and another there, with the redemption of some individual drunkard, thief, or adulterer: that was not his character. He was strong, energetic, commanding: his voice was imperative in condemnation of evil and of unbelief, and forceful in exhortation to confess Christ, and be clean.

But General Booth did more. He made his work permanent, and extended it to every part of the planet, among all nations and all peoples. He was not only an eloquent missioner, he was also a great organizer—in fact, a man of statesmanlike genius as well as a simple follower of Christ. He saw his first little companies grow into regiments, brigades, and army corps. For the workless, shops were needed; for the sick, hospitals; for the services, chapels; for the army, headquarters. All these grew under his direction and skill: and they sprang up everywhere to meet the needs of a new church, a church universal, that did not invite proselytes, but sought out the victims of woe and disaster and vice, and converted them, not to be members of a new church or soldiers of a non-militant crusading army, but to see themselves in their true relation as children of God.

General Booth gathered the unfit into his army, not to poison their minds against the fit, as the godless and cruel self-appointed leaders of the "proletariat" have done, but, on the contrary, to make them fit companions for those whose lot has been cast in pleasanter places. With the example and the sayings of his Master always in his mind, he realized the enormous importance of the command, "Render unto Cæsar the things that are Cæsar's, and unto God the things that are God's." He well knew that without Cæsar's aid his work would soon come to an end among the penniless unfit, and he was much too wise, and I may say too godly, to give a moment's notice to the vapourings of foolish men whose prime doctrine is a denial of Christ and the elimination of God from the affairs of life.

General Booth was not a visionary, and he was not a social reformer. He was an evangelist of the old-fashioned type, as vigorous as Saint Peter, and as wise as Saint Paul. Woe unto the Salvation Army should one of its leaders become a social reformer!

The work of General Booth had the effect of a leaven in that part of society which had fallen into want and despondency. It is only necessary to ask the question, What would have been the state of England if this leaven had not been introduced? to realize the enormous good that has been effected by the energy and activity of the members of the Army.
One day, while walking with Major Perry up and down the platform at Hadley Wood Station, the Major described to me the redemption from the lowest depths of moral and physical degradation of several men who had become prominent, useful, and trustworthy officers in the Army. He laid so much stress upon the possibility of reclaiming the worst men, that I at last was led to say that it seemed to be almost necessary to be, at first, a great sinner in order to become a great saint. The Major did not seem to relish this way of putting the matter, but in the end had to admit a grain of truth in it.
As the train did not arrive, we discussed the characteristics of human nature at great length, without being completely in agreement upon its principles. He could easily persuade me that generous, easy-going, and strongly emotional spirits could be led astray and subsequently recovered, but nothing would convince me that certain kinds of predatory natures ever could be changed.
To-day the ordinary man, who is neither all good nor all bad, is asking himself if a great increase in over-good men would not be a greater danger to the State than an increase in bad men. It would be so much easier to deal with bad men than with some of our lofty idealists.
The first time I painted General Booth he gave me several long sittings. He was widely experienced in world affairs, and as he had travelled extensively, and moved freely among men of many nations, creeds, and stations, his conversation was interesting and unrestrained. His was a commanding personality, and he was as positive in his opinions as he was fearless in expressing them. On hearing that I had one son, he said inquiringly, "An artist, like yourself, I suppose?" "No," I replied, "he is an astronomer." "Worse and worse!" he exclaimed, with a degree of surprise and alarm in his voice, and continued by declaiming against astronomy and all astronomers, stigmatizing the science as one of the most useless on the whole useless list. "It was not God's intention that we should have any knowledge of the sun, moon, and stars," he went on earnestly, and he professed a conviction that no one knew anything of any real importance about the heavens!
He invited me to join him and Commissioner Kitching at tea. After saying grace he turned sharply to me and asked, "Why don't you say 'Amen'? Say 'Amen'! I murmured that I had said "Amen," to which he replied that "Amen" should be said in a loud and grateful voice, and not muttered under the breath. I glanced nervously at the young orderly who was serving the buns and the cakes, and was consoled to see that he looked just a little

scared on my account.

The General was very abstemious, too much so for his own good. The food he was taking—bread and tea, or perhaps an egg, was not sufficient to make blood, and I found him pale and far from strong.

The next time I went to paint at Hadley Wood a great change had taken place. Weakness had increased, but a beautiful pallor in the skin harmonized with the white and wonderful hair and beard of my sitter. I looked forward with delight to the opportunity of making a study of his fine head: but he was restless, and now and again forgot that he was sitting for his portrait. I worked with feverish haste, and almost blindly, in order to get something, but soon was disturbed by an orderly who opened the door to tell me that my train would be at the station in ten minutes. I paid no attention, but worked on until he came again, with almost a command in his voice, and then I hastily put the canvas against the wall, without even looking at it, and believing it to be nothing worth, hurried off to the train, after an abrupt adieu.

The General died a few days later. Some months afterwards I received a letter from Commissioner Kitching asking me to call at the headquarters in the city. I was ushered into the room of the new General, who showed me the sketch I had made of his father, with which he was well pleased. It was a revelation to me, for I had not worked more than twenty minutes at it, and with many interruptions.

When I heard of General Booth's death I suggested that a cast should be taken of his features; but a feeling of delicacy, which I shared, caused the family to hesitate upon a step which seemed to them more or less sacrilegious; so I proposed to take clay and model the mask, which, of course, could be done without touching the face of the dead.

The General was lying in state in the northern part of London; and it was arranged that, on the eve of the funeral, after all the mourners had had a last view of their beloved leader, I should go to this tabernacle at midnight, and work as long as I liked. It was then late in the evening, and I had no clay. It was with considerable difficulty that I obtained enough from John Swan for my purpose. Starting on the long drive from home, I reached the great audience hall about midnight. Entering the building, I looked down a long flight of steps upon a strange scene. In the centre, far below, a black bier supported the remains of the General; four sentinels stood, silent and motionless, at each corner.

Descending the staircase, I moved up to the platform and took my place beside the corpse of the majestic old man, and began to work. Presently a great fatigue overcame me: and as dawn began to appear I staggered under the burden of the clay image in my arms, up the long flight of steps to the open air, and almost falling into the cab, sank down exhausted upon the cushions, from which the coachman aroused me an hour later when the first rays of the sun were beginning to close the pale petals of the evening primroses in the garden.

THE PUBLISHER

MY most vivid recollection of the Publisher is when I was trying to climb on his shoulders, at the risk of plunging into the square below, while he was leaning out of an upper window of the Johnson House to see a Zeppelin passing that was dropping bombs. The police were shouting at us, and threatening to raid the house, if we did not go in and turn out the lights. The great airship was slowly sailing overhead, brilliantly illuminated by the flare of the searchlights and the explosion of shells, and as we were a company of twenty-eight in the upper room just under the roof, a chance bomb falling upon the house would, in all probability, have shattered the majority of us.

The Publisher had kindly invited me to be his guest at a supper of the Johnson Club. At supper Mr. Clement Shorter sat on my right, Mr. Augustine Birrell just beyond him, and a group of members of Parliament were sitting around the secretary at the head of the table and opposite to us. After supper a paper was read on the cynicism of Dr. Johnson. Before the discussion began the secretary was asked to look in the dictionary to find the precise definition of a cynic. While he was doing so, a loud explosion was heard outside and near by. I did not recognize the sound; it was very loud, but dull, and did not reverberate: so I turned to Clement Shorter to say that a Zeppelin raid was in progress, when another and nearer explosion confirmed my suspicions; and a remarkable change in Mr. Shorter's complexion and expression made it evident that he also realized the situation. A very pronounced increase in the beat of my heart, and the colour, or the lack of it, of a tall man opposite, who had risen, as most of us were doing, caused me to search for the signs of an emotion of fright: but all that I found was that of an intense feeling of curiosity to see the airship, a curiosity that I had never known before, and which became so powerful, that in the struggle to get up on the Publisher's back—he had been quicker to reach the window than I—I almost precipitated both of us into Gough Square.

"Oh!" we all groaned in varying notes of surprise, alarm, and execration, as the thing passed immediately over us, sailing eastward. It was very high, and soon disappeared, although a little man beside me persisted in saying he could still see it; and when I suggested that he only saw the Pleiades through the thin veil of smoke, he resentfully remarked that it was the Zeppelin, because he had often seen airships manoeuvring at night over Lake Constance. The police had now become so insistent, that we reluctantly left the window, and retook our seats at table to discuss "the cynicism of Dr. Johnson."

Birrell, I think, led off, and thirteen others took part in the debate. Half an hour after the raid a visitor would not have discovered in the calm of our procedure that anything unusual had happened. The porch of the Lyceum Theatre had been blown up, a drinking house opposite partly destroyed, and a number of people killed. The Morning Post building was on fire, and all the windows in that part of Fleet Street and the Strand blown out. When we left the Johnson House, at eleven o'clock, I looked up at the constellation of stars which my neighbour at the window took for the retreating Zeppelin, and as he passed me I said, "Do you see the Pleiades?" To which he responded in an aggrieved tone, "Yes, yes." In Fleet Street we walked through what seemed to be masses of broken ice, and stood for a few minutes watching the firemen on ladders against the Morning Post building, putting out the fire. There I left the Publisher, thanking him for his kind and novel entertainment, and proceeded across the bridge to Waterloo Station.

The lights were out, soldiers and others were lying about, and no trains were running. Hurrying to the underground I took a train to Richmond, that was redirected to Ealing on the way, and got down somewhere at 2 a.m. A kind policeman roused up a man from his bed, who drove me in a taxi to The Hermitage, which I reached at three o'clock, to the great relief of my family. This was the first air raid. During the two long years which followed, they were so frequent that they became a commonplace thing to the Publisher and his wife, who, from their windows in Adelphi Terrace, had a free view of the ships and planes that flew up and down the Thames every moonlit night.

The day after the supper in Gough Square I came into London to see the effect of the raid upon the people. The Strand and Fleet Street were densely crowded with sightseers on foot, gaping in wonderment at the havoc that had been made. Less than half a mile away, in Oxford Street, the traffic was going on as usual, and the pavements were crowded with shoppers, who either did not know, or did not care, that a murderous and destructive raid had taken place.

I first met the Publisher at No. 14, Buckingham Street, Strand, long the residence of Joseph and Mrs. Pennell, whose hospitality to fellow-craftsmen and to publishers and Pressmen was proverbial. I found in the Publisher a pronounced Free Trader, a warm disciple of his father-in-law, Richard Cobden; and as he was also a member of various Liberal Clubs, I thought him a trifle distant, and that he no doubt suspected me of being a Protectionist and a Conservative.

Old parties have been riven asunder by the war, and old names have given place to new ones. "Unionist" is no more, and if "Conservative" and "Labour" still remain like embers of dying causes, "Profiteer" and "Proletaire" are more popular. The things themselves still exist as faculties of government, but the names, as expressions of theories or doctrines, have been discarded for Internationalism, Proletariat, the World State, and other glorified denominations that are intended first to dress out human nature in a garb of common mediocrity, and then gradually to reduce man to the condition of the ants and the bees.

These advanced doctrines have both alarmed us and drawn us closer together, as, happily, most men of integrity and goodwill have been gathered into a solid phalanx to defend themselves from the complots of schemers, who have conjured up a mirage of illusions to tempt the foolish and covetous. In addition to the weaknesses of human nature, the variable climate of this planet makes the realization of every Utopian idea impossible.

Two portraits of the Publisher were painted—one in his old-fashioned Adam room, at No. 1, Adelphi Terrace, and the other at The Hermitage. When Mrs. Cobden Unwin saw the first portrait, she was as frank as Mrs. "Colonel" House, and said, "I do not like it—it's all lavender." In one thing the Publisher is conservative. His clothes are the colour of lavender; and this tint is enhanced by a yellow necktie that is perpetually renewed. In the second portrait I avoided lavender, and succeeded in pleasing Mrs. Cobden Unwin with tones of brown and gray.

The sittings at The Hermitage were enlivened by amusing talks about men and women who appear in books; and as the Publisher has had many opportunities for the study of authors, as well as of the people they write about, I have made mental notes for a volume of "Studio Causeries." These talks, whilst he sat for me, to pass the time, and perhaps keep him from going to sleep, led him to reveal some of the experiences of his profession; and it was interesting to me, as an American, to find his wide knowledge of American publishers and literary men, which he seems to have obtained during the last forty years or more. In the middle 'eighties he became the publisher of The Century and St. Nicholas magazines, which at that time, and for a good many years, were two of the best American periodicals; and they contained work by many of his and my friends, both artists and literary men. Joseph Pennell and his wife, both of whom I have painted, were great contributors to these magazines, and they were naturally acquainted with the Publisher; and I gathered they frequently met, and sometimes on the scenes of the artist's work. For instance, when Pennell was doing his English Cathedrals they spent week-ends together at Canterbury, Gloucester, and Ely; at the latter place, apparently, the Publisher had to go down to help the artist out of some copyright trouble with the local photographer, who was inclined to assume that the artist could not draw the cathedral without his help. Then again he was with Pennell when he was drawing The Oldest Church in London, St. Bartholomew's the Great, and again at Chelsea; these pictures eventually took book form. The book on Chelsea was written by Dr. Martin, another American, who collaborated with Lawrence Hutton, known to his friends as "Uncle Larry," in that good book Literary Landmarks of London.

Another suggestion for articles, which came, apparently, from the Publisher, was a visit to the Thames. The Publisher, with Mr. and Mrs. Pennell and other friends, paddled from Oxford to Kingston. The result of this excursion was issued under the title of The Stream of Pleasure.

Again and again they must have met in Paris for the opening of the Salon: Mrs. Pennell at that time wrote her well-known articles on Art for the New York Nation under the initials N. N. On one of these visits a party of artists and critics discovered in the shop of a picture-framer in Montmartre a large collection of paintings by Van Gogh, which must have been given by the artist in payment for paints and brushes. Only one of the party, the Publisher, dared to speculate with a few sovereigns. These masterpieces are now sold for hundreds and even thousands of pounds. If only the party had been wiser, even if worse critics!

JOSEPH PENNELL

THE names of three great Quakers are associated with the city of Philadelphia. William Penn, the founder, who well deserved to transmit his name to the beautiful state, Pennsylvania, of which Philadelphia is the chief city, is well known to every school boy and girl, who, if they have not seen his sturdy and Friend-like figure in the picture of the Treaty Tree, can see it every day, perched high, in rather incongruous fashion, on the tower of the City Hall.

The second great Quaker was Benjamin West, whose name is not so well known by the school-children, or even adult citizens of Philadelphia. In time, when his work is better appreciated by the custodians of Art, and when his masterpieces that are now "skied" almost out of sight in the Pennsylvania Academy of the Fine Arts, are loyally placed in a Benjamin West gallery in the Municipal Art Museum, the good citizens will learn to appreciate the great talents of one who, though born in the precincts of Swarthmore, received full recognition of his genius in England, and who was elected by his fellow-artists President of the Royal Academy of London.

I well remember an engraved portrait of Benjamin West that hung in the dining-room of my father's house. It was placed opposite an engraved portrait of Washington, after the painting by Gilbert Stuart. My father was an admirer of West and his work, and in this way showed his respect and esteem for a great American.

The third Quaker is Joseph Pennell. He, like West, has found in England and in Europe a more congenial field for the exercise of his talents; but in spite of his long residence in London, unlike West he has remained an American and, above all, a Philadelphian. Penn and West were English Quakers; Pennell is an American Quaker, and proud of his association with the Society of Friends, in love with the old meeting-houses, and in complete sympathy with the pacific tenets and ideas of the society. Naturally of a soft and gentle disposition, he can sometimes, when his artistic instincts are violated, be aroused to vehement opposition, almost to aggressiveness, in the pursuit of his pet theories; and, like all Quakers, he believes he is right.

At an early period in his career, with his wife, Elizabeth Robins Pennell, a helpmeet and coadjutor whom Heaven must have designed for him, he began to traverse Europe in search of the picturesque; and after finding numerous imperfect specimens which were brilliantly and artistically recorded, with both pen and pencil, he found the real thing—the most picturesque town in the world—Le Puy, in mid-France.

On one occasion Fisher Unwin and Pennell met in Provence—this was while the artist was drawing those wonderful cloisters in the cathedral at Arles. There was some trouble with the Gens d'Armes, as the artist would sketch near the fortifications protecting Les Saintes Maries on the Bouche du Rhône. This journey resulted in a great picture, for, on leaving the artist, Fisher Unwin got off the train at a town called Le Puy and wrote to Pennell that he must come there and sketch; and so later in The Century an article appeared entitled "The Most Picturesque Place in the World." Many wrote asking its name and where it was. Besides the article in that magazine, Pennell made one or two of his most famous etchings of that picturesque old French town.

Fisher Unwin spent some time at Zermatt with Mr. and Mrs. Pennell: and there Pennell sketched and climbed. Unwin's idea was that the artist's black-and-white work was perhaps the most satisfactory medium of obtaining the grandeur and simplicity of Alpine effects.

In the course of these wanderings Pennell made drawings of almost every cathedral and cathedral town in Italy, in Spain, in France, in Germany, and in the Low Countries. And Central Europe at one time—Hungary, the Balkans—supplied him with rich and abundant material for his prolific pencil.

Throughout his life Pennell has been a keen and tireless worker. He found in England an inexhaustible mine of architectural beauty. His pencil, his etching needle, or, finally, his lithographic crayon, were always in that wonderful left hand, a hand endowed with swiftness and accuracy in expressing, on paper, on copper, or on stone, the visions of an eye and a mind so sensitive to proportion that he has been able adequately to render, with a few bold lines, the grandeur of an edifice or of some sublime fabric in Nature.

I well remember a lecture at the Adelphi, when Pennell was asked if his lithographs of the Panama Canal did not give an exaggerated idea of the height and depth of the cuttings, because no photographs gave the same impression of bigness. A member of the audience rose and said, "Pennell's drawings are true, and give the right proportions of the cuttings; the photographs are false."

In the same manner his drawings of the streets of New York have given the scale to all other painters and draughtsmen who have attempted, in most cases vainly, to represent the monstrous modern city. He has also presented the abnormal vastness of the Canyon of the Colorado River, and suggested in a simple and masterly fashion the temples and terraces of imaginary barbarous Babylons, that seem to grow out of the hazy, opalescent mists of that great crack in the earth's surface. I also remember a lithograph of the mound of earth at the entrance to the Fairmount Park, the site of the old city reservoir, which always reminded me of the Acropolis of Athens.

Lithography soon began to absorb the attention and tireless energy of the artist. Under the stimulus of Whistler, whose experiments on stone and paper had given to lithography a delicacy, a subtlety, and a refinement of execution before unknown, Pennell himself began to study the process of drawing on paper without previous preparation, and the methods of transference to the stone which obtained the best results. In a very short time he had not only discovered the tricks of the trade, but uncovered them, condemning many as useless, and adding others of his own invention which he found to be simple and helpful. A study of the origin and progress of the art led to the publication of Lithography and Lithographers, by Joseph Pennell and E. Robins Pennell, the first volume of a graphic art series. It was published by T. Fisher Unwin in 1915. In this valuable work the history of the art of lithography is traced from its inventor, or "finder," as the German has it, Alois Senefelder, to the present time. It is a comprehensive story of lithography requiring endless research and nice discrimination in the selection of the hundreds of examples given in the pages.

The publication of this work gave a great impetus to the practice of lithography, and enlarged the taste of the public for an art that had fallen into disuse, save for commercial purposes. Pennell gathered around him a few men eager to pursue an attractive method of producing unlimited replicas of their drawings, and he formed the Senefelder Club, and was elected its first president. The artists and art societies and the museums of England and Europe were aroused to the importance of lithography among the fine arts, and Pennell was delighted to find that he could exercise his gifts of organization in developing one of the graphic arts, and in helping the draughtsmen who appealed to him for assistance from Paris, and Rome, and Venice, and Leipzig.

His authority and influence became from that time universal; and it is a remarkable tribute to his power for work that he was able to cope with a correspondence that threatened seriously to interfere with his work as etcher, lithographer, and author. One can only marvel at his powers of endurance; for, in addition to the various tasks of the day, his lavish hospitality and the time he allotted to his friends in the evening are frankly betrayed in Nights, that delightful account by Mrs. Pennell, of the "talk" of friends who gathered around a board whereon the most savoury of provençal dishes were placed by that inimitable cordon bleu, Augustine, for the delectation of Henley, Bobbie Ross, Fisher Unwin, Bob Stevenson, and a host of other literary lights, or darks, as the case might be.

Pennell was now constantly in demand by the Governments of England, France, Italy, and Germany, to make lithographic drawings, as artistic documents of reference of their great industrial works: and prior to, and during the war he was in communication with Ministers of War and Lords of the Admiralty, who desired drawings of navy yards, battleships and cruisers, munition works and gun factories. His life became intensely amusing, as he would say, for he daily met men of all ranks, in the army and navy, who knew what guns and ships were, but who did not know anything about Art. In the end, when America declared war, he had to leave his beloved Thames, which he overlooked from the many windows of his wonderful atelier in the Adelphi quarter. The Zeppelins had increased in number and in the frequency of their visits, and the flare of the searchlights, the flashing of anti-aircraft guns, the bursting of bombs, all of which were plainly visible from his high point of vantage, or disadvantage, gave him the most thrilling effects for the exercise of his genius.

In America, Pennell found fresh opportunities for the display of his energies. The American Government, like the English and French, employed him to make drawings of the battleships, of the munition works, and armament factories, and to assist in advertising the war loans. He threw himself into the work with enthusiasm and zeal, giving his time and his talent, without remuneration, to the printing and distribution of war posters throughout the land.

No one in the country excelled this Anglo-American Quaker in enthusiasm and self-sacrifice in aiding the American Government and the people in that critical time. In order to procure the sinews of war, he displayed throughout the Union a series of lithographs illustrating, in imaginative as well as realistic fashion, the creation of monster guns, monster locomotives, and monster ships. His theme had long been "the wonders of work," and he now could fulfil his gospel as the chief missioner "of the power and beauty of labour."

Finally, the world of Art is grateful to him for having written the life of the most subtle, the most refined, and at the same time the most direct of modern artists—an etcher and a painter without a peer, James McNeil Whistler. It can rarely be said of a modern artist that he belongs to the world; of Whistler and Pennell it may truthfully be affirmed, and of Pennell it may be added that he has made the world his own.

EDWARD H. COATES

I PAINTED Mr. Coates the first time in Camp Elsinore, on the wild shores of Lake Saint Regis, in the Adirondack Mountains. It was an ideal spot for work or, it would be more just to say, for idleness. The warm, pine-scented air invited you to rest, and the still, clear water lured you to float on its surface in a birch-bark canoe.

But Mr. Coates, seated on the piazza, made an attractive picture: so I gathered my brushes into my hand and sketched him as he sat with his pet dog on his knee—a study in black and gray. This was the most interesting portrait of the three that were painted. The second was done in Murestead, when he and Mrs. Coates were making us a visit in London. The third was made in camp, during the third year of the war. Hidden away among the pines, in those peaceful mountains, the echoes of the conflict were very faint; for at that time America was only engaged in sending munitions to the Allies, and was not assisting them in the field.

There is a mystery in the charm of the north-woods which belongs to a time that antedates the life of man. Here man has left little trace of himself: and as one wanders northward, tracks are almost lost in the forests that are covered deep in moss. From these lands, from the great mountains of the West, and from the boundless deserts and prairies, the "cry of the wild" comes forth, the cry that, once heard, is never silent in the heart of him who loves the virgin soil, untouched by the heel of man—the cry that comes only out of the solitudes of America. With that cry ringing softly in my ears, I painted and I dreamed, and often at my side a soft and gentle voice breathed this song—

Friendship from its moorings strays,
 Love binds fast together;

Friendship is for balmy days,
Love for stormy weather.

For itself the one contends
Fancied wrongs regretting—
Love the thing it loves defends,
All besides forgetting.

Friendship is the morning lark
Toward the sunrise winging,
Love the nightingale, at dark
Most divinely singing!

The reign of Mr. Coates at the Academy marked the period of its greatest prosperity. Rich endowments were made to the schools, a gallery of national portraiture was formed, and some of the best examples of Gilbert Stuart's work acquired. The annual exhibitions attained a brilliancy and éclat hitherto unknown. Two of the greatest masterpieces of American Art were produced—The Clinic of Doctor Gross and The Clinic of Dr. Agnew, by Thomas Eakins—rare works that carry on the best traditions of the masters. Unfortunately, it may be said in parentheses, these pictures are hidden away, one in the University of Pennsylvania, and the other in the College of Medicine, where the public has little opportunity to see and study them.

World-renowned American masters of Art were, at this time, in the hey-day of their success, and the walls of the Academy were annually adorned by important works from the hands of Sargent, Abbey, Whistler, Cecilia Beaux, Chase, Anschutz, Tanner, Weir, Lawson, Twatchman, and a host of brilliant young painters rising into fame.

Mr. Coates wisely established the schools upon a conservative basis, building almost unconsciously the dykes high against the oncoming flow of insane novelties in art patterns, and keeping the pumps going against the ebb that was carrying the weak-minded and feeble-fingered back to the totems of Yucatan and Kamschatka. In this last struggle against modernism the President was ably supported by Eakins, Anschutz, Grafly, Thouron, Vonnoh, and Chase.

His unfailing courtesy, his disinterested thoughtfulness, his tactfulness, and his modesty endeared him to scholars and masters alike. No sacrifice of time or of means was too great, if he thought he could accomplish the end he always had in view—the honour and the glory of the Academy. It was under Mr. Coates' enlightened direction that was fulfilled the expressed wish of Benjamin West, the first honorary Academician, that "Philadelphia may be as much celebrated for her galleries of paintings by the native genius of the country, as she is distinguished by the virtues of her people; and that she may be looked up to as the Athens of the Western World in all that can give polish to the human mind."

In the interests of the Academy Mr. Coates became a generous patron of the arts: and it was not difficult, to one of his affable and persuasive nature, to enlist the hearty sympathy and the generous financial support of many of his colleagues and fellow-trustees. A marked feature of his administration, and one which assured its success, was the happy faculty of drawing around him advisers chosen from the ranks of the artists themselves. I can look back with a feeling of pleasure to the thought that I may have been partly instrumental in obtaining for the winners of the travelling scholarships an increased grant from the Cresson Fund, to enable the student to live decently, as well as comfortably, in Paris or in Rome. It was at an interview which I had with Mr. Coates upon this subject that I earnestly brought to the attention of the President the great truth that the creation of artists was not so important as their maintenance. And I pointed out very forcibly the cruel mistake of an over-inducement, through money prizes, to many young persons to enter a profession in which patronage was exceedingly limited, and in which success is usually more illusory and elusive than in any other. Artists can make themselves, but at the outset none can maintain himself without aid.

DR WEIR MITCHELL

THE city of Philadelphia was at one time renowned for its School of Medicine. Students flocked there from all parts of America to attend the clinics of surgeons like Dr. Agnew and Dr. Gross. And these two distinguished anatomists found their Rembrandt in a contemporary artist, Thomas Eakins, whose masterly delineation of their clinics compares favourably with that of the famous Lessons in Anatomy, in Amsterdam.

It was to be expected that a man of Weir Mitchell's imaginative and poetic temperament would select that branch of medical science which gives greater play to the metaphysical faculties than the more exact practice of surgery. His early student days coincided with the first investigations by the new school of neurologists into temperament; and psychology, as a new word to describe an old but until then little-considered thing, was bandied about in hospital and theatre, in ballroom and sickroom. The treatment of the alimentary canal gave place to the study of the spinal cord. Neurosis and neurasthenia explained all the disorders of the dyspeptic.

Dr. Mitchell was by inclination a naturalist: whether through premeditation or predestination, knowingly or ignorantly, he took Aristotle for his guide. The aristocratic principle, that supports all the arguments of the Greek philosopher, was readily accepted and adapted to the life and the researches of the young neurologist. He quickly diagnosed the state of society, and the habits of the animals suggested a cure that could be applied to each individual. Men and women have been overcome by two gnawing human desires which feverishly they sought to gratify—love of money and love of pleasure. The mental excitement and fatigue attendant upon such questionable pursuits enfeebled the body and wrecked the nerves.

As a keen student of morals, the young doctor quickly perceived that theologians, on the one hand, had ever conspired to divide immortal man from the "beasts that perish," and, on the other, social reformers ignored the teachings of nature in constructing their artificial codes of social ethics. In both systems man is treated either as a spiritual or a mental entity, entirely regardless of his physical nature.

The young scientist hit upon the plan of treating the animal part of man as the animal treated itself. Having discovered that for the greater part of the day all animate nature is in repose, he instituted among his patients a system whereby continuous rest became obligatory. To exhausted men he said, "If you wish to live, go kill something"; to women with shattered nerves, "You must hibernate." The pursuit of game became a tonic for men; long hours of sleep soothed ambitious and aspiring women, and restored their balance. The proof of the accuracy of his diagnosis lay in the success of the treatment prescribed. As a naturalist and pathologist his fame was secure.

He next turned his attention to the study of the venom of reptiles, and, in collaboration with Dr. John Madison Taylor, published the results of his investigations into the effects of their bites.

His artistic temperament found expression in poetic and prose writings, whose interest and merit may in time surpass, in men's memories, his achievements in science. Sentiment often lives longer than empiricism.

DR JOHN MADISON TAYLOR

AS a youth John was an athlete. Between him and George Fox, of Andalusia, there existed that friendly rivalry in feats of strength and agility that urged them to take advantage of every opportunity for training their bodies in athletic exercise. Thus they reached a degree of perfection rarely attained by professional athletes, for the simple reason that the latter usually specialize and over-develop certain muscles at the expense of others. Nature had endowed these young men with unusual beauty of form which is rare among well-developed and strong men. Muscular development on a frame that is not built upon the graceful and conventional lines of the Greek model may express force without creating in the mind an emotion of beauty. Correctness of proportion in length of torso and limb is not even sufficient. The muscles must be formed and attached in the way they are found in the best specimens of Grecian sculpture, for the Greeks aimed at perfecting their bodies in beauty as much as or perhaps more than in strength.

The Greek sculptors, taking advantage of their opportunities of studying the figures of the best athletes, who were constantly exposed to their view undisfigured by the indecencies of dress, arrived at a rendering of the human figure, sometimes realistic, sometimes typical, which marks the place and the period of man's highest development. And it is worthy of note that the Greeks had arrived at a knowledge of the value of repose, for action is rare in their Art. Nearly all their statues are presented in repose. The expression on the faces of their gods is placid. Passion was not permitted to distort the features. No matter how their literature may represent the gods to have been moved to anger, to hate, to love, or to jealousy, no faint trace of this must be allowed to distort their classic features, or produce an ungraceful curve in mouth or brow. A godlike serenity of countenance displays the calm which ought to reign within. In the Greek plays grief and despair are veiled from public view by drawing the robe across the face. Our modern actors seek the approbation of the audience by their skill in displaying fright and anger, and the Japanese are past-masters in working themselves by slow degrees into a white passion that ends by the most extravagant divergence of the eyes in their sockets, in writhings of the mouth, and other unpleasant symptoms of human degradation.

My recollections of John Taylor at the age of twenty years recall more vividly now than they impressed me at the time the peculiar similarity that he showed, not to any particular Greek character perhaps, but to the general Greek type, although the similarity was made more conspicuous by a quite unique resemblance to the Antinous in the regular character of the features, the shape of the head, and the growth of the hair. Resemblances between men have always interested me more than differences and contrasts: but one must confess that men, even of the same race, vary to a degree almost unbelievable, until specimens of the varieties are placed side by side. The misfortune is that men resemble each other more frequently in ugliness than in beauty, and in passing I may say that the ugliness is increasing, if not in degree, certainly in number. The cult of the beautiful and the noble belongs to the religious age, the age of worship, of veneration, of respect, of loyalty, of fidelity—all the qualities that are now often mocked at and despised. Beauty can be cultivated as flowers are: and it was cultivated in the times gone by when women were content to be women, and not freakish men. That old supercherie of Jacob's when he played the trick on Laban, his father-in-law, by placing parti-coloured withes before the ewes, is a well-known pathological, rather than psychological, manifestation of the effect, through the eyes, either for good or for ill upon the unborn. There is nothing more elevating to the human mind than the aspect of things that appeal to the emotion of beauty, either in the music of running water, the fragrance of flowers, or the blue of the sky. He who has known how a feeling of the most profound depression gives place to elation when a day dawns that vibrates with a musical twang in wind and sky, in rustling trees and rippling river, although the cause for depression still exists, can understand the mystical relation between cause and effect in the transmission of beautiful forms into beautiful thoughts. No one knows better than Dr. Taylor the disastrous effect upon mankind of neglecting those aids to health and beauty which are to be found in the right stimulation of the senses and the well-ordered indulgence in the emotions. There is a pathological side to all manifestations of life—to this side Dr. Taylor gives unremitting observation and attention. He is the convinced advocate of what some people would call a theory, but which nevertheless is a fact, that the mental constitution and equipment of one-fifth of the inhabitants of a nation render them unfit for the ordinary performance of civic duties, that, in consequence, any extension of liberty in the direction of communism is impossible. The whole basis of the communistic theory resting as it does upon a false notion of equality in mental and physical powers, that basis does not exist and will not exist so long as disease and insanity afflict mankind. States, like ships, are built for storms and wars, and not for calm seas or peaceful peoples. And furthermore no one has, as yet, seemed to realize that the variable climates of this planet are unsuited to the Utopian notions of our so numerous visionaries and vagabonds.

One of the most interesting fields of research entered by Dr. Taylor led him to many important discoveries concerning the effects of poisoning by snake-bites. He associated himself with Dr. Weir Mitchell, who in collaboration with him investigated the character and intensity of various poisons in the different species of venomous reptiles, and the antidotes to each. The picturesque Mount Desert Island was chosen by both scientists for the pursuit of their studies, an island which, in some respects, resembles in character some of the beauty spots of the old world.

When the portrait was painted, Dr. Taylor had changed from the appearance of the Greek athlete to the more usual type of the man of science. There are still traces of the classical lineaments, which we all admired in the youth, to be seen in the fine profile; and although the hair is gone, and already the effects of reading and study begin to appear, the old love of sport and of athletic exercise still lingers in a frame that retains all the vigour of youth. The Maine woods and the silent lakes of Canada are the happy hunting-grounds of the idle moments of a man who lives in the open and breathes deeply of the health-laden air of mountain and forest.

LORD HALSBURY

I PAINTED Lord Halsbury among a group of Lords Justices of Appeal sitting in the old Court of Appeal that has been for some time past used as a writing and reading room for counsel.

This chamber constituted one of the most dignified and imposing Courts in the great building at Temple Bar. Its severe and simple character, the bench arched over by a wooden frame, surmounted by the Lion and the Unicorn, which enclosed the Lords Justices and protected them from draughts, made a solemn impression upon me when I first entered it. Their lordships in their full-bottom wigs and watered-silk robes trimmed with gold lace had the effect of being separated from the rest of the world by an atmosphere of mystery of peculiar picturesqueness.

Lord Halsbury was at that time Lord Chancellor, and presided over the court. The attitudes of the Lords Justices seemed to vary according to their rank, the chief among them, the president, the Master of the Rolls, Lord Esher, and Lord Justice Lindley, being very much at their ease, especially the latter, whose wig was always awry, and half concealing a very red face; while those at the two ends of the bench sat upright, wearing their robes with less abandon.

My interest had been aroused first in Lord Halsbury long before, when, as Sir Hardinge Gifford, he was counsel for the plaintiffs in the case Belt versus Lawes. The whole gist of the case was, Can a sculptor issue to the public comparatively indifferent work without being suspected of employing "ghosts" to do it for him? The action should not have been brought. Belt's subsequent conduct leads one to suppose that he expected substantial damages from the defendant, a sculptor whose father was a wealthy man. What the witnesses for the defendant, including the President of the Royal Academy and other artist members, could not see was that the work produced by Belt was of such a commonplace character, that anyone with an atom of ability could easily have done it all, therefore Belt could have done his own work, even if he did employ other men to assist him.

I had a studio next to Belt's, and was in the habit of visiting him frequently to watch the progress of a bust of Lord Beaconsfield, a good likeness, I imagine, but executed in a hard, tight manner. Perhaps he was fooling me, and only pretending to put his little pellets of clay on a head that had already been modelled by one of the "ghosts"; but as he modelled in court, during the trial, a bust that was kept under lock and key when he was not working on it, one must infer that a real spirit helped him, or else that one of those he employed obtained access to the room in which it was locked when the court was not sitting. The jury was satisfied that they saw the clay shaped and fashioned before their eyes into a semblance of the model, and so was I. But it took forty days to decide that a man of ordinary talent could easily model in clay without producing a work of genius. It is customary for busy sculptors to employ men to assist them, modellers, carvers, chisellers, metal workers, etc. The Austrian sculptor Boehm, who possessed no extraordinary ability, employed, I was informed, the young French sculptor Dallou, who was an artist of great talent, if not genius.

If some of Dallou's brilliant touches appeared on the tails and manes of the horses, on their hocks and pasterns, it is not likely that Boehm would have conscientiously cut them out. These assistants become "ghosts" only when their skill exceeds that of their employers.

Many years after this episode, when Sir Hardinge Gifford had taken his seat on the Woolsack as Lord Halsbury, and presided over the law lords who heard the cases that were referred to the House of Lords, Mr. Hugh Capron was dining at Murestead, and during the evening asked if I had seen in the papers the notice of the decision of the House of Lords on the Scottish Church case. He was surprised to hear me answer "No," and to follow it by asking what it was about. Shortly he recounted the story—how, on a point of doctrine, a small body of clergy and their scanty followers in some of the outlying northern islands of Scotland, had seceded from the body of the Free Church of Scotland, and had laid claim to all the property of the Church, including many millions in funds, all the schools, church buildings and colleges, and pursued that claim into the courts of Scotland, where they had been non-suited on several appeals, and how, not satisfied with the decision in their own courts, they had carried their case to the House of Lords, and there had obtained a reversion of the decisions in the courts in Scotland, and a verdict which carried with it the title to the vast property of the main body of the Church. After hearing this tale, to which Capron added that the Lord Chancellor Halsbury had delivered a weighty argument in favour of the "Wee Frees," as they were called, based on the dogmatism of certain seventeenth-century divines in Holland on Predestination and

Free Will, I said, "That decision will require an Act of Parliament to undo." For the first time, and for a time, I found myself in disagreement with Lord Halsbury, whose career, both judicial and political, I had followed with close attention and interest; and yet I could not restrain a feeling of admiration for a man who was so loyal in his maintenance of a legal principle as to sacrifice justice and right to a point of law involving itself both justice and right. No doubt the "Wee Frees" were in the right as regards the existing legal conditions. Two years afterwards Parliament destroyed the effect of the decision by special enactment.

But this is not the only time that Lord Halsbury supported a minority. If in the first instance he was a consistent supporter on legal grounds of the "Wee Frees," he was in the end a consistent and logical champion of the "Die Hards" and their cause. The two cases were analogous in the gravity and importance of their underlying principles. The "Wee Frees" and the "Die Hards" held tenaciously to tradition; their opponents, in a vast majority, threw tradition and prestige and principles to the winds. The "Wee Frees" rested their claim on the ground that right makes might; the "Die Hards" fought, not for themselves, but for a majority that sought to divest itself from tradition and voluntarily to renounce privilege and power. Twenty-two stalwart peers, with Lord Halsbury as their champion and leader, resisted by every argument that loyal conservatism and constitutional authority could suggest the suicidal proposal to "reform" the House of Lords.

Lord Halsbury had said to me that success at the Bar, and in the political arena, depended very much upon physical strength, upon the power to endure strain and fatigue. That it was so in his case is evident, for he was eighty-five years of age when this unequal struggle in the Upper Chamber, to prevent it from destroying itself, was maintained by a gallant band of twenty-two against six hundred.

Lord Willoughby de Broke was an active lieutenant and aide to Lord Halsbury. He organized meetings with the object of obtaining the moral support of the country against this proposal of self-immolation; and the Morning Post, ever and always the mouthpiece of Conservatism, eloquently supported his efforts. To me the situation was interesting historically and philosophically. The philosophy of government is second only in importance to the practice of Art. There is no such thing as a philosophy of Art, for it is not governed by changeable principles. It is based on unchangeable Nature: Art is a thing to be taken for granted, government is not.

There is but one form of government, whatever the name given to it—monarchy, oligarchy, or republic; there is no such thing as an autocracy or a democracy: the people cannot rule because of their plurality, and an autocrat cannot rule because of his "singularity." In a so-called "autocracy" there is a delegation of power from above; in a "democracy" a delegation of power from below—the many elect a few; the one selects many; and neither the one nor the other can know how much or how often their confidence will be abused.

After many experiments in the arrangement of government in ancient and mediæval times, the Mother of Parliaments decided that the best provision for good government was a constitutional sovereign, with the power of advice only, and two Houses, an upper and a lower, the first hereditary and nominative, the second elective, with certain well-defined powers, the most important being the right of veto by the House of Lords.

The government of the United States was established upon the same principle, under a written Constitution. The House of Representatives holds the position of the House of Commons, the Senate corresponds to the House of Lords, the President and his Cabinet to the Prime Minister and his Ministers. One element is lacking, the sovereign. The system is entirely elective, excepting in the case of the members of the Cabinet, who are nominated by the President. The government of the United States is consequently incomplete, because there is no spiritual head to whom all the people can be loyally attached. But there is one paramount power in the government of the Republic—the Senate: while in England the Second Chamber has already been divested of its powers, and the Commons are fast losing their authority, and autocratic procedure is being usurped by Prime Ministers, the Senate of the United States is reaffirming its rights and privileges under the Constitution, and becoming more potent for good every day. And it would be strange indeed if a nation that organized its government on the principle of rule by the delegates of the people should allow one delegate, even though he be the chief magistrate, to arrogate to himself a preponderating influence in either internal or foreign affairs. In a crisis it may be well for one man to possess almost dictatorial powers, but it is a healthier and saner sign when counsels emanate from the council chamber, and not from the cabinet of the roi de fait.

The following letters were published in the Pall Mall Gazette. Ten years later it is not uninstructive to contrast the strength of the Second Chamber in America with the weakness of the Second Chamber in England.

With a shrieking multitude outside demanding the abolishment of every institution on which civilization is based, including literature and art, it is a little difficult to write rationally or temperately; but encouragement and hope can be found in the reported words of President Harding, addressed to the officers and sailors recently from the deck of the battleship Pennsylvania: "The United States of America does not want a thing on earth which does not rightfully belong to us—no territory, no payment of tribute—but we do want that which is righteously our own, and by the Eternal we mean to have it."

LORD HALSBURY.
To the Editor of the Pall Mall Gazette.

SIR,
It may be well to consider for a moment the qualifications of the man who seems to be destined to save the Constitution of this country from disgrace and ruin.
Lord Halsbury led the minority of seventeen Peers who voted against Lord Rosebery's resolution to abolish the hereditary privilege. In doing so, he simply recognized that man should not be deprived of the benefits which have accrued to him through the working of the laws of nature. His bold and defiant courage at the age of eighty-six is miraculous and awful. His career at the Bar, on the Bench, and on the Woolsack entitle him to the respect and obedience of his fellow-men.
As Lord Chancellor he was the Speaker of the House of Lords during a greater number of years than any of his compeers, and is, therefore, thoroughly competent to lead the House.
As a jurist of nearly sixty years' experience, he is able to defend, with integrity of purpose and singleness of aim, the functions of the second estate of the Realm from the attacks of sycophants and traitors, and the betrayal of cowards.

Yours, etc.,
CONSTITUTIONALIST.

July 25, 1910.
Pall Mall Gazette.

HOUSE OF LORDS REFORM.
To the Editor of the Pall Mall Gazette.

SIR,
The attitude of a portion of the Unionist Press, and of some of the Peers themselves, towards the hereditary principle is far more surprising than the periodical outbursts of defeated Radicals and Socialists against the restraining influence and the usefulness of a Second Chamber. The latter is but the legacy of the extremists in the first congress of the colonists of America and of the revolutionaries in France; the former can only come from a latent fear that concessions to the mob may be necessary to preserve the fabric of the Constitution from decay and ruin.
It might possibly have been wiser, unquestionably it would have been both politic and magnanimous, on the part of the autocrat Tsar of Russia to have

listened favourably to the petition of his clamouring subjects on that fateful Sunday morning when they begged loudly for a measure of political freedom; but for Unionists and Royalists to join voices with Socialists and Radicals in the outcry against the most enlightened form of government the world has yet seen, or will ever be likely to see, displays an unpardonable ignorance of history and of human nature.

Consider the Republic of the United States after one hundred and twenty years of trial. The counsels of Thomas Jefferson, the democrat, prevailed over the more subtle insight and foresight of Alexander Hamilton—whose statecraft was estimated more highly by Talleyrand than Napoleon's or Washington's—with the result that aristocratical and hereditary principles were rigorously excluded from the Constitution. In compensation for this exclusion a logical regard for the principle of natural fitness has made the office of Senator almost an office for life, whereby veteran Senators, through repeated re-elections, have been forced, quite naturally, into the aristocratical position; it is only another step to the hereditary. So much for political evolution.

It may now be asked, In what does the Republican system excel the English Monarchical system? No one can truthfully affirm that the temporary President of the United States receives the same degree of loyalty from the two political parties, or from the people at large, as the King of England receives from his subjects: or that the House of Representatives is superior, by the integrity and ability of its members, to the British House of Commons: or that the Senate is as reserved in its legislative action as the House of Lords.

Weigh both systems in the balance, and at once it will be seen that it is not the principle of natural selection—which is hereditary—but the system of artificial election that will be found wanting.

There can be no more certainty of obtaining five hundred good legislators by election than by birth, and the advantages of birth and wealth in the composition of a Second Chamber are clearly shown in a sentence quoted by a former correspondent from Oliver's Life of Alexander Hamilton. It will bear repetition: "His aim was economic: Popular government may secure at a cheap price the services of a large number of men in easy circumstances, of superior education, and of family traditions of loyal service to the State."

Yours faithfully,
J. McLure Hamilton.

February 22, 1910.

THE SINGLE CHAMBER AND ITS DANGERS.

To the Editor of the Pall Mall Gazette.

SIR,

In his speech at Burnley on December 5th Mr. Asquith laid great stress upon the fact that the Veto of the Crown had been dead for two hundred years: and he followed the statement by asking his audience if the country had been any the worse without it. At the present juncture it might be reasonably urged that the government of the country could be better conducted by restoring the function of this technical part of the law of the land.

On the occasion of the inaugural dinner of the Agenda Club, at the Hotel Cecil, my neighbour—a young man—coolly remarked that an autocratic monarch could best solve the problems which are now baffling the ingenuity of both political parties: that party government was no longer either efficient or useful.

This may possibly be an extreme view, but it shows that the reaction against the proposed tyranny of an absolute Single Chamber is violent, and likely to be far-reaching in its effects.

All moderate men should not forget that the framers of the Constitution of the Republic of the United States were not beguiled by democrats of the Jeffersonian type into any such error as Single Chamber government. After long and careful consideration of all known Constitutions, both ancient and modern, they adopted the well-tried system of Great Britain, diminishing nothing, but adding to the fabric the safeguard of the President's veto.

Section 7 of this Constitution reads:—

1. All bills for raising revenue shall originate in the House of Representatives, but the Senate may propose or concur with amendments, as on other bills.
2. Every bill which shall have passed the House of Representatives and the Senate shall, before it becomes a law, be presented to the President of the United States. If he approve, he shall sign it, but if not, he shall return it, with his objections, to that House in which it shall have originated, who shall enter the objections at large on their journal, and proceed to reconsider it. If after such reconsideration two-thirds of that House shall agree to pass the bill, it shall be sent, together with the objections, to the other House, by which it shall likewise be reconsidered, and, if approved by two-thirds of that House, it shall become a law.

Here we have no less than three checks to hasty legislation. And be it also remarked that to pass a bill into a law over the veto of the President a two-thirds majority of both Houses is requisite.

Yours, etc.,
CONSTITUTIONALIST.

December 9, 1910.

CHARLES MARQUEDANT BURNS

I HAVE always associated Charley Burns with two friends of similar tastes and distastes—Henry Thouron and Robert Arthur. Three of us could often have been found together, but rarely all four. Although there was a great harmony between any two of us, when four were assembled discords began that led to embarrassment. Thouron held positive views on subjects which Burns and Arthur ignored completely, while I, being more catholic in disposition, held dissolving views upon many questions, and strong opinions only upon essentials.

Charles Burns is the youngest old man I have ever known, for although he is eighty-two, his capacity for enjoyment seems to be unlimited. Whenever I feel the need for rejuvenation, I seek him out for my cicerone.

There is only one thing upon which Burns is silent—his achievements in architecture. On all other subjects he is even garrulous. In our frequent journeyings together over Europe and in England, he has been an instructive companion on all matters connected with Gothic cathedrals. Had he been as communicative upon the creation of edifices in America from plans inspired by his own genius, it would have been an inspiring subject. But his genius far exceeded his opportunities. From an early age he had absorbed a knowledge of the masterpieces of Gothic architecture in Europe, but his ambition to put that knowledge into practice had little hope of gratification in America, where no religious community had at that time the taste or the means to build that costliest of all structures—a Gothic cathedral.

His performances having, perforce, fallen far short of his ideals, he became obsessed with the idea that his achievements were so unworthy of comparison with the masterpieces of the great Gothic period in Europe that he made no effort to make them known. Nevertheless, in the history of

American church-building, Charles M. Burns stands out as the designer of the best example of Gothic architecture in the country prior to the end of the nineteenth century.

This chaste specimen of his work is the South Memorial Church that stands in Diamond Street, west of Broad Street, Philadelphia. The interior is remarkable for the purity and simplicity of its lines, and for the extraordinary impression of grandeur produced by the architect's innate sense of proportion. The church is a model of elegance and of fidelity to the spirit of French Gothic.

Mr. Frank Darley, the well-known organist, invited our architect to remodel his house in Broad Street, which was so well done that at the death of the owner it was purchased by the great jurist, Mr. John G. Johnson, for his remarkable collection of Old Masters. It was Mr. Johnson's intention to make this house a permanent gallery of paintings for the city of Philadelphia; but the genius of the advocate overreached itself in the making of his own will, which was so involved in legal phraseology of an indeterminate character, that it admitted a construction that was far removed from the intention of the donor. Through a lack of foresight on the part of Mr. Johnson, a charming old garden adjoining the house, which, had it been secured to the property, would have provided against any future need for expansion, was allowed to be sacrificed to the base uses of commerce. With a little thought and a moderate expenditure the Johnson house might have become the home of another Wallace Collection, and South Broad Street redeemed in part from the slough into which it has been allowed to sink.

Travellers with an observant sense for the beautiful, going between New York and Philadelphia, may have been struck with the design of an old-world-looking building, near Torresdale, on the right of the railway, which in autumn is covered with rust-coloured creeping vines that harmonize with the tone of the structure. This convent is also Burns' design: and it would not be surprising to discover that when, throughout the length and breadth of the land, some unusually picturesque bit of architecture comes into view, it is the handiwork of that matchless builder, Charles Marquedant Burns.

He arrived years before his country was ready to receive him, before the field was cleared of the horrors of the "Centennial" period. It was Burns who ploughed the field and prepared the soil; and he has lived long enough to see younger men reap the harvest.

He might have been first among the husbandmen, had he not been the pioneer of Gothic renaissance in America.

GEORGE F. WATTS

AS I opened the door of Signor's large studio in Melbury Road one morning I may have sneezed. A voice from the far end of the long room called out, "You have a cold! If you come in I shall catch it, and keep it all winter; do please go home; and come again when you are well." Calling back "Good-bye," I left the house, filled with admiration for a man who knew how to protect himself at the expense of ceremony, the gift that charms when the sun shines, but is always ridiculous when it rains.

Signor, as his pet name implies, was an Italian in everything but nativity. Throughout his career he was the artist in dress, in manner, and in temperament, among princely patrons. He lived and thought and worked upon a plane elevated above that of other men—even of Leighton and Burne-Jones, whose ideals surpassed those of their contemporaries.

When I first knew him he was white-haired, and always dressed in a long, gray coat that gave him the look of a painter of the Cinquecento. There are interesting photographs, but no characteristic painting, of one of the most picturesque figures of the nineteenth century. I was only able to obtain a pastel drawing that is now in the collection of Mr. Edward H. Coates.

As Signor was a spiritual son of Italy in the Middle Ages, and a material child of modern England, he often found himself perplexed by the problems that are vexing society in the present, and darkening the outlook into the future. His nobility of purpose and his goodness of heart obscured his vision. His best portrait is probably that of a Socialist, Walter Crane.

JUDGE ALEXANDER SIMPSON

AS I grow older the advantages of having been born an American of British and French blood become daily more and more ideal. I now know that I have escaped the insulating influences and the national prejudices of all three countries, and have retained only their qualities—chiefly good. I have been poised, as it were, high over the Atlantic Ocean, from which exalted vantage point my eye could encompass, in its wide sweep, Penn's tower in Philadelphia, Wren's cathedral in London, and the church of Notre-Dame in Paris.

My father's liberal spirit provided against the possibility of any such Americanism as conceives Virginia to be a Garden of Eden and George and Martha Washington a sort of political Adam and Eve. Although, in some ways, I owe England so much, I cherish fondly a kind of super-liberty of thought which I could have derived from no other soil than that of America. America, populous and powerful as she has suddenly become, still retains the instincts and the virtues of a small and primitive society. In the beginning of her history three forces for good operated as incentives to right thought and action—Puritanism, Quakerism, and Republicanism.

By the latter word neither a form of government nor a political party is meant, but simply the public good, morally, socially, and politically.

The influence of Puritans and Friends was not so general as the restraining virtue of the idea contained in pro bono publico that permeated the Thirteen Original Colonies at the time of the Declaration of Independence, and swayed the states as they entered the union. The best men said to themselves, "To deserve a pure government we must keep society pure." And what did that entail? Two things, one of which has unfortunately fallen into disuse—obedience to law, human and divine, and the swift execution of justice upon evildoers. In this atmosphere of stern realities, men of the

temper of Judge Alexander Simpson and my father were born.
Like the curate who was considered, by the toddy-drinking, "churchwarden"-smoking old Scotsman, of no use to man or beast because he did not drink, smoke, or eat hay, men of the type of the Judge and my father, who refused the Masonic grip, rejected the flowing bowl, and eschewed Dame Nicotine in any shape or form, are of little use in clubs or at artists' banquets, but when some real service to the community is to be performed, either by example or precept, they can be depended upon with all confidence to do their duty. The likeness between the two natures extends almost indefinitely. At the back of their minds they believe in a Christian Church universal, they love England and her institutions, they are loyal to the Constitution of the United States, and read it in all its simplicity of statement; they hold visionaries and demagogues in detestation, their knowledge of psychology does not go beyond Saint Paul's or Shakespeare's, their sentiment is a pure substantive and their goodness is not a pious pose.
Judge Simpson is a leader of these men of substance, whose feet are firmly planted upon the inviolable principles of human nature, guided by God's Word. His chief characteristic is decision, based upon a comprehensive knowledge of truth. His faith is unlimited. Writing of the "back-washes" of the recent conflict in Europe, he says "I cannot, however, get up even a measure of alarm over it, so far as England is concerned, her people are so staid and sensible; their instincts are so just and right; their traditions and their modern performances are so inspiring, that I look to see a gradual adjustment through a number of years, perhaps fewer than now seem possible, and then a settling down to the handling of her imperial problems as only English-thinking people can handle them."
Unlike another great American jurist, who possessed one similar taste, Judge Simpson is very human. In the gratification of his taste for Art he considers both his compatriots and his contemporaries; he collects modern pictures by Americans. To collect a few fine examples of ancient painting for the decoration of houses, like Mr. Frick's, in New York, or Mr. Widener's, in Philadelphia, is no doubt justifiable on grounds more or less personal; but to gather together a mass of canvases of considerable æsthetic value and pack them away out of sight denotes a mind of inferior sensibility. It may meet the approbation of a few American artists, both sculptors and painters, if it be urged that it is the office of museums to collect old Art, and a duty incumbent upon individuals to patronize living artists. That we owe the existence of the great masterpieces of ancient Art to contemporary patronage is merely to state the obvious.
It is to the deep and steady undercurrent of thought flowing from the minds of men like Judge Simpson that America owes her position to-day as a power for good.

JUDGE WILLIAM W. PORTER

AFTER leaving the Matilija Canyon, where I had a delightful fortnight, fishing the rainbow trout in company with Birge Harrison, Mrs. Harrison, my wife and son, and a philanthropic social reformer, Anna Farnsworth, I wandered slowly up the State of California to Monterey, San Francisco, the Shasta Springs. I had a fully matured intention of continuing northwards to Vancouver, and perhaps to Alaska, and had only arrived in Portland, Oregon, when a letter containing an urgent appeal to return at once to Philadelphia reached me from William W. Porter, an attorney-at-law. I was informed of certain transactions that had taken place, and I was asked, in the public interest, to commence a contest in the courts to right a wrong. The wrong was both apparent and real; yet after a long and detailed conversation with Mr. Porter, to whom I hurried, I told him that he might enter me as a plaintiff, but that the case was lost already, because we had not a foot to stand upon. Mr. Porter differed from me; but the sequel proved that I was right. The case was tried before three courts, and each time it went against us—the last time on Washington's birthday, when the court, as a great favour to us, consented to forgo the holiday and hear counsel's pleadings. Mr. Porter on that occasion displayed all his eloquence, his power of acute and logical reasoning, his innuendo, and after the end of his argument left the court quivering with emotion—and fatigue! I knew by the expressions on the faces of the judges, the presiding one of the three being the judge who had decided against us in the first instance, that the brilliant display of sound reasoning had been of no avail, and that the verdict would be a confirmation of that of the court below. The court sat, if I am not in error, in the old historic State House; and on leaving it we walked silently across Independence Square. Counsel for the defendants had been, to my mind, too leniently dealt with. Court etiquette had been punctiliously observed and the bona fides of the opposing attorney tacitly accepted, whereas his evidence, had it been sufficiently sifted, might have caused a change of view on the part of two of the judges. Thoughtlessly, with my mind centred upon the point, I impulsively broke the silence by saying, "I wish I could have conducted the case myself." Porter was profoundly hurt, never more so perhaps in his legal career: but I have always felt that he knew the words I had uttered implied nothing more than a censure on exaggerated professional etiquette which, among doctors and lawyers, must be obeyed, though a man bleed to death, or be hung innocently in consequence. The friendship that had sprung up between us as a result of our long consultations upon the various points of the case was proof against a blow even so severe as that which I had inadvertently given and of which he felt only the glancing force. I aimed at a bad custom. Porter's conduct of the case had been perfect, every argument for and against had been sifted and examined with the minutest circumspection: but custom drew a veil over the only vulnerable point in the defendant's armour.

And then I painted his portrait, which hurt him and vexed him far more than my random remark! It was painted after he became Judge of the Supreme Court of Pennsylvania.

He sat in his private room in the Public Buildings overlooking Broad Street, as it extended southwards to the Delaware River. The light was not good, and the sun often bothered me. The result was so unsatisfactory that on the evening of the reception at the Academy, as I was talking with Dr. John Taylor and my wife, the Doctor turned and, seeing the portrait across the large gallery, said, "Oh, look! who painted that awful thing of Judge Porter?"

His work on the bench soon became too sedentary for a man of Judge Porter's tastes. Life in the open air suited his robust constitution and active mind. He soon realized that writing opinions on uninteresting points of law in opposition to those of his colleagues was somewhat tame and monotonous in comparison to the forensic displays between opposing counsel on the floor of the court: and he yearned for his former life in the fields among his horses and cattle. He loved above all other things to be a country gentleman. Among the hills of northern Jersey the contemplation of the growing corn and wheat upon his broad acres gave him more pleasure than following the complexities of the law, and trying to make them accord with equity and justice. Here the weather and the weevil often caused him apprehension: but when the sun shone he could turn to his beloved horses, admire their well-groomed coats, watch their paces, and speculate upon the prospects of the geldings and mares.

His chief joy was to mount the box-seat of his coach and, glancing admiringly at four powerful bays, while taking the ribbons and whip in his hand, tool them at a spanking trot through the hedge-grown lanes and over the turnpike roads which, in those days, were free from the motor that has made the elegant and exhilarating pastime of driving high-strung and restive horses almost obsolete.

Judge Porter's traditional love of horses has been inherited by his daughter, who, like Margot, can ride straight to hounds.

There are two subjects on which Judge Porter dissents from me, Art and Finance, and no amount of threshing out by both of us will ever separate the wheat from the chaff. He will admit that wheat is for use and flowers for beauty, but not that the latter is as important in the economy of things as the former; from my point of view more important, because they stand for æsthetics and ethics, the same sentiments being innate in both; whereas wheat, a mere accident in life, or the result of a misfortune in Eden, is the remnant of a rudimentary state of man, and does not go to the root of civilization as flowers do.

At our first, or one of our first, interviews he was led by some remark of mine to say, "Oh! Art is only an accident in life." It was said with a judicial manner, as he was poring over a brief, and with a tone of finality.

With ars longa vita brevis in mind, I said, "I should like to argue that point with you. To me Art seems the only normal thing, whereas law and medicine are merely the results of the accidents of life." The Judge was taken aback at this attack upon the professions, and, plunging deeper into his papers, muttered, "Impossible; but I am too busy to argue it now." That subject has been a closed book between us ever since. A man of his acumen could not fail to see that I was right, for a broken heart, a broken leg, or a lost cause brought law or surgery into being, while Art and flowers flourished on earth long before Cain killed Abel, or Moses received the Tables of the law; they are coeval with the blue and starry heavens.

But on the score of finance we are irreconcilable. A true disciple of Adam Smith, the Judge will persist in contemplating wealth in terms of bricks and mortar, while my contention is that wealth today is merely a written promise to pay, based on earning capacity. He and his school say that shells burst in warfare are not only wealth wasted, but wealth destroyers. While admitting that they destroy life and property, they serve the same purpose as wealth producers as flowers do that are sold by the florist at ten dollars a dozen, and in a day or two are blown away and consigned to the dustbin. But the florist has booked them, just as Dupont books his powder and shot; and if we trace back to its source the labour expended upon raw materials in the production of flowers and shells, we shall be astonished at the similarity of the steps and processes involved. Before 1914 the Chancellor of the Exchequer found it difficult to raise for his Budget the sum of two hundred millions of pounds. To-day the surplus is more than that, and the revenue required is one billion of pounds—think of it! five billions of dollars! Where did it come from? From making shells and guns, boots and shoes, and food—all of which have been consumed by soldiers, and of which some broken remnants are dumped about, marring the landscape. That money could have built a hundred marble cities roofed in gold. It still is there on books as debts—for some men thought, and other men worked for it. Most wealth is earned by men who think and men who serve, not merely by men who labour with their hands to produce bricks, mortar, and houses. And the men who serve, be they waiters in a café, or priests, or doctors, or lawyers, are the most numerous. Karl Marx put his tongue in his cheek when he wrote Das Kapital—and he did worse, for he threw a lighted bituminous torch into an inflammable mass that, once set on fire, can never be extinguished. But I am forgetting that when Judge Porter, a master of repartee, whose parries are skilful—though his riposte is still better—and I last fenced with these foils, the seconds never cried touché once.

THE REV. STEPHEN GLADSTONE

WHEN I first began to paint Mr. Gladstone, at Hawarden, Mrs. Drew would often invite me in the afternoons to visit with her the different places of interest in the neighbourhood. Her daughter, Dossie, the fair-haired child whose picture at that period was on a page of every illustrated newspaper in the kingdom, and beyond it, presented me to her pet black Pomeranian puppy, and together we would seek out her father, Canon Drew, in the midst of his books and papers, and beguile him into taking a walk in the gardens or the park.

It was natural that these walks should sometimes end at the Rectory, where the "Rector," Mr. Gladstone's familiar title in Hawarden, and Mrs. Gladstone, surrounded by their family of sturdy sons and a daughter, would welcome us to tea. The baby of the house was then about two years old. His brow was remarkable for a child, and the head resembled his grandfather's, even to the thin fringe of blond hair that hung and curled behind like the soft, gray locks of the old statesman. I could not help predicting a great career for him. He now lies, like his cousin William of Hawarden, among the brave youths who fell in the battle-fields of France.

Stephen Gladstone was more like his father than any of the members of the family. He was tall and powerfully built, with a physique capable of any amount of endurance or fatigue. Many years after this, when painting Mrs. Gladstone at Manley Hall, I heard that the Rector had walked from Bangor to Hawarden, more than sixty miles, in one day, when in his sixty-first year, as though to show that his resignation from the parish of Hawarden had no connection with any physical failure. In his youth he performed a similar feat of endurance, when, as an Oxford undergraduate, without any special training, he walked the fifty-four miles between Oxford and London in one day. Those who started with him dropped off, as the pace was four miles an hour.

The reproduction is from a hasty sketch. The Rector had promised to come to The Hermitage and sit for his portrait, but a sudden illness carried him away before the promise could be fulfilled.

HENRY E. GLADSTONE

WHEN writing of Mr. Gladstone I referred to the two preoccupations of his life, the State and his family. It would be difficult to say which held the first place in his mind; and he may never have asked that question of himself. In the light of present-day advanced (?) thought it would not be impossible to give to the family again its rightful place. The State is not an entity, as some theorists would make us believe, but an abstraction only. It is to society what currency is to trade, a convenience and nothing more. It may be very truly said that a perfect statesman gives his head to the State, and his heart to his family. By so doing he will gather the double reward of gratitude from the people whom he served with his head, and the affection of the family to whom he gave his heart.

When his powers were nearly spent, and his dominant self-reliance almost gone, Mr. Gladstone found in his third son, Henry, a pillar of strength upon whom he could lean with that complete abandonment of self that bespeaks perfect confidence as well as affection. How many times in the year the voice of one of the family rang out from the little church at Hawarden the command and promise, "Honour thy father and thy mother, that thy days may be long in the land which the Lord thy God giveth thee"! If ever a command were obeyed and a promise fulfilled it was here, where the conviction was inborn that obedience from a people to this commandment assured the stability of the State, and gave the true key-note to society.

As the promise was not fulfilled in the case of the heir to Hawarden, William Glynne Charles Gladstone, who gave "youth's brief fiery blow for Freedom," and fell on the battle-fields of France, the castle and estate devolved upon his uncle, Mr. Henry E. Gladstone, the Lord-Lieutenant of Cheshire.

In this official capacity I painted him. With all the grace, charm, and good-humour imaginable, he gave me sittings at The Hermitage in order that I might in the easiest and pleasantest manner accomplish the work. The sittings were enlivened by the relation of amusing incidents that had occurred in the home and field, for the Lord-Lieutenant is like his brother, Lord Gladstone, an ardent sportsman.

WILLIAM G. C. GLADSTONE

THE youth of England that survived the battle-fields has been shaken and shattered, either in body or in mind; those who were too young to fight are bewildered by the aftermath of the war. Most of those who fought and those who stood by and watched are finding a solace in sport, and it is well for them and the future generation that in innocent physical exercises they discover a happy alternative to the social and political game now being played.

When Browning wrote—

Our men scarce seem in earnest now.
Distinguished names? And yet somehow,
It seems as if they played at names
Still more distinguished, like the games of children,—

he foresaw the games continuing into the future, and played with false earnestness and hidden motives.

One youth there was who, had he survived, would have re-entered the political game to fight for fair-play and for upright and honest dealing.

But the Master of Hawarden, the brilliant heir of an illustrious grandfather, a shining young Parliamentarian, was allowed through some fateful error to risk his life and lose it uselessly, though honourably, as a soldier, when his civic virtues and talents entitled him to permanent usefulness in the Council Chamber.

The youth is gone, and old men carry on the game undisturbed and unperturbed.

CANON ARMOUR

AS I sat one Sunday morning on one of the front side benches of the English Church in that little citta of the Italian Riviera whose name sounds like a joyous sigh—Alassio!—there kneeled in front of me a surpliced clergyman, so unusual a presence that it was with a mind turned to various reflections that I heard him reading the service, which he did in a rich and expressive voice.

He personified, as few men do, the majesty of manhood, and that thought inspired me with another which seemed to be its corollary, the majesty of England. For what other land could have produced so noble a son? Had he been a youth, the echo of Pope Gregory the Great's exclamation, "Non Angli sed angeli," would have reached me, but he was a man on the verge of seventy years, as powerful and robust as in his prime, untouched by Father Time or the finger of Care. And then my mind began to wander away from the church to take a general survey of the race from which this stalwart giant had sprung, and I could see his forefathers battling against the Saracens; on the fields of Flanders with Marlborough, on English soil when Cavalier and Roundhead struggled for supremacy, or in distant lands across the seas seeking fortune and, while in the search, unwittingly building up the foundations of the Empire. And then I saw them again spreading themselves over the earth seeking rest and pleasure and health in all the beauty spots where the orange blossomed, and the palm threw out its arched fronds, and the sun blazed kindly on their red bronze cheeks.

And wherever I saw them they were a race apart from all the others; almost as distinct from the Latin or the Slav or the Teuton in bearing and dress, as they were from the Oriental who knows them as the British Sahibs. On the Riviera from Hyères to Capri they have built their villas and their churches; on the Nile and in the Desert, in Ceylon, and in far-away Hong Kong, and by the shores of the Pacific, from San Diego to Vancouver, these cool-headed and warm-blooded islanders seek a climate that stirs a blood too often chilled by the fogs of their own land.

This is a race of men that stands alone among other peoples, isolated in a throng of twenty different nationalities whose chief characteristic is their resemblance one to another. What is the secret of this individuality? When was it brought about, and how?

In the enchanting garden of Costa Lupara, more beautiful, I thought, than La Mortala, Canon Armour often walked with me on the terraces, where through the gray-green olive-leaves the silver-blue sea sparkled like flashes of light from the facets of millions of gems, telling me of the glories of his own dear England, of its loyal and faithful sons and daughters. He, who had seen generation after generation of boys grow to manhood under his guidance at the Merchant Taylors' School in Liverpool, where he had been head master for forty years, could testify with pride, almost paternal, to the nobility of the youths he had had such a large part in training to be worthy of an Empire whose history was emblazoned as brilliantly by conquests in science in times of peace as by feats of arms in war.

And when war came, this confidence in the manhood of the Empire was gloriously justified; and my aged friend, not to be outdone by younger men, resolved to do his part. In his seventy-sixth year he undertook the duties and burdens of the parish of Berkeley in Gloucestershire, one among the very large parishes of England, of which his son was the Vicar, in order that the son might be free to serve as a Chaplain at the front. Canon Armour continued his ministrations until his son's return at the end of the war, resigning them in the eightieth year of his age.

Among the many men I have known, Canon Armour possesses in a remarkable degree what a writer has attributed to La Fontaine, "that gracious common-sense, founded on a courageous acceptance of the realities of life, and at the same time inspired and lightened by imagination and poesy." The true mystic is often a very efficient and practical man of affairs; and in Canon Armour the spiritual side of life is closely interwoven with the fabric of the material. In homely phrase, "he is a man first, and a parson afterwards." If I were to express truthfully his thought, I am persuaded it would be that true spirituality finds its roots in the necessities of our material nature, and blossoms more gracefully where these necessities are naturally and legitimately gratified.

EDWARD CLIFFORD

EDWARD CLIFFORD'S life presented one of those human problems for which there seems to be no solution: a paradox which, on analysis, might prove to be no paradox at all. He was born to be an evangelist, but an evangelist of an unusual type, and outside and apart from any Church or sect. Although he worked for years before his death as the secretary of the Church Army, an institution that had modelled itself partially on the pattern of the Salvation Army, he was, I believe, not otherwise allied to the Anglican Church, but esteemed himself as of Christ, and not of Paul, or of Apollos, or of Cephas.

Unlike his Divine Master, who sought His disciples among the lowly and the humble, the missionary efforts of Edward Clifford were directed to the regeneration of the wealthy and the noble. Bearing in mind the saying that it is easier for a camel to go through the eye of a needle than for a rich man to enter into the Kingdom of God, he opened his studio—for Clifford was an artist as well as an evangelist—to those members of the aristocracy who had been awakened to an interest in spiritual things by attending the Mildmay Conferences organized by Lord and Lady Mount Temple. Many Americans were attracted to these conferences, among them Mr. and Mrs. Robert Pearsall Smith. Hannah Smith was a "perfectionist" and an able expounder of the Prophets who had commenced her career in Philadelphia by giving drawing-room readings of the Scriptures.

When I was first taken by Walter Tyndale to one of these readings in Clifford's studio I was surprised to meet Hannah Smith, whom I had known in Germantown and Philadelphia as a reader at meetings in my aunt's house, where I sometimes made long visits when a boy. This unexpected meeting brought to mind an amusing incident at one of these readings, when Hannah ended a rather long prayer by asking the Lord to remind Mrs. Mercer of the shawl she had promised her, my aunt, at the moment of the petition, being on her knees not more than four feet away from the petitioner.

Clifford loved gardens and flowers passionately. He sought out the most beautiful old and historical gardens in the country and made drawings of them. He had a curious way of arranging flowers in his rooms. Instead of clustering them into bunches or bouquets, he would place fine specimens of roses, carnations, or dahlias singly in long-stemmed glasses in rows along the mantelpieces, or crowd a table with them.

The generation now passing away remembers him as the historian of Father Damien, the self-sacrificing and devoted priest, who immolated himself among the lepers in the hope of improving and brightening their hard lot and inspiring them with hope of a future and better existence.

DAVID CROAL THOMSON

THE little portrait of Cosmo Monkhouse, about which Herkomer was so indiscreet in the opinion of Onslow Ford, procured for me a commission from one whose approbation and patronage was dearer to me than any other. David Croal Thomson had already won for himself a premier position among connoisseurs and writers on Art. His intimate knowledge of the various schools of modern Art, which was soon to include a comprehensive view of old painting, and particularly of the masterly English School that thrived under the Georges, and died under Victoria, singled him out as a man eminently fitted to be the historian of the Barbizon School, and of the Modern Dutch School, as he, indirectly, includes its story with that of the brothers Maris—James, Matthew, and William. It is, perhaps, wrong to say that the history of the school is indirectly given in the story of these three painters, because they, with the addition of Mauve, Israels, and Bosboom, express directly the character and achievement of the school.

Even though Croal Thomson may not consider Art hereditary as a matter of course, it is yet interesting to note that he traces downwards from the Old Dutch artists—Ruysdael, Hobbema, and Van der Neer, the English Bonnington, Constable, and Turner, and the Modern French—Daubigny, Corot, and Harpignies. It would be as difficult to prove that Art is hereditary—unless the Japanese artists are proof of it—as to prove, on the Darwinian hypothesis, that physical individual characteristics are inherited and pass from father to son. But it may be said without much fear of contradiction that Art is traditional, and is, unfortunately perhaps, liable to lapses. In Spain Art has fallen from the height which it attained with the ascendancy of Zurbaran and Velasquez, and in Italy from the time when Uccello, Crevelli, Titian, and Veronese held their glorious sway. In fact all

Art between the time of Phidias and that of Michael Angelo suffered an ever-increasing eclipse, until Botticelli and Giotto opened the windows anew to a ray of light, which again was shut out before the close of the sixteenth century, to remain extinguished until our own time.

All great Art—I am speaking now of painting—centres around the year 1600. A few names will show that, with the exception of the Van Eycks, who came just a little before them, the great painters of the Low Countries, of Italy, and of Spain, lived in the same period. Franz Hals, Rembrandt, Rubens, Van Dyck, Raphael, Titian, and other Italians too numerous to mention, and the Spaniard Velasquez, were contemporaneous painters, and great painting expired with them. The English are the only artists that have revived the tradition: and strange enough it is to have to relate that before this revival, which came through Sir Joshua Reynolds, Gainsborough, Romney, Raeburn, Gilbert Stuart, and Benjamin West, the English had produced Hogarth only.

About the time of the end of the reign of the Georges this great revived tradition died again in England, and remained dead until the French Manet took up the threads, and, handling them in a very imperfect way, passed them on to Carolus Duran, and he, not knowing how to weave them into his work, passed them to John Sargent, whose brilliant dexterity almost realized the traditions of 1600. If Sir John Millais had not joined the pre-Raphaelites, who knows what he might have accomplished in great painting? Whistler, Charles Furse, and Thomas Eakins, each in his own way, carried on the traditions for a few years; but there are already signs of another relapse that may prove fatal.

The inspiration of all really great Art, as Ruskin so wisely points out, is religion. Another three centuries may see the end of that—communism and religion cannot exist together. Art in some form, either great or small, lives as a tradition through all the ages, building, either well or ill, upon that which was already laid in varying strata, as civilization proceeded. It has never been spontaneous, and never can be. That this is so can be discovered from an examination of the illustrations of Matthew Mans' work in Croal Thomson's book, which plainly indicate that he blossomed from many grafts upon the same tree. In particular, Cottage Scene shows, if not the German ancestry of his family, the direct influence of German Art, of a period anterior to Menzel; at other times the blossom is the result of a graft from his brother James, and again from William. He is at his best when he is pursuing his own fantasies, his day-dreams of princes and princesses and castles in the air, pictorial expressions of that inner and spiritual life that was in such contrast to his real and bitter experience.

We often wonder if there is a mathematical law governing the phenomena of coincidences. They are so mysterious, and sometimes so startling, as to induce a belief in a direct personal intention. Like Francis Bacon's, my own fateful number seems to be fifty-three. It was on the lintel of the door leading into the grounds of Hawarden Castle when I first sought my way there to paint Mr. Gladstone. It is chiselled on a stone inserted in the wall of the garden of The Hermitage; and if ever I write of the houses I have lived in, it will be shown how coincidences have led me to decide upon buying or leasing them. No. 8, Henrietta Street, had always been known to me as Vine House, where my old friend, Henrietta Hind, lived and cultivated a vine which bore such small, neat, and compact bunches of grapes that I at first thought the vine was artificial; so like painted, hammered iron it seemed to be. On the wall, in the hall, Henrietta had hung a large bunch of grapes, carved in wood, to carry on the raison d'être of the name. When, after an absence of two or three years, I found the name changed to Barbizon House, and my old friend and patron, D. Croal Thomson, installed there among a collection of drawings by Brabazon Brabazon, that clever artist who knew how to breathe on to paper in puffs of coloured smoke the most charming skies and lakes, and mountains and Venetian palaces, I began to wonder what magic carpet had effected the harmonious transformation.

Mr. Thomson greeted me with his well-known, genial smile, and took me through all the familiar rooms. He invited me to show the portraits of "Colonel" House I had painted at the Hotel Crillon in Paris, and with great generosity placed the rooms at my disposal. He was full of anecdotes about himself and his strange experiences with artists and doctors, some of which I cannot discreetly divulge. But there is one that so generously displays his love of fair criticism that it must be recorded. A letter had appeared in the columns of the American Art News, disparaging the work of Duveneck, who had received a special gold medal at the request of the international jurors for his exhibition of portraits and pictures at the Panama-Pacific Exposition, at San Francisco, in 1915—an honour unique in character, and spontaneously offered in recognition of his unusual talents. Mr. Thomson had seen Duveneck's work, in Cincinnati, some time before this, and admired it. With the feeling that an injustice had been done a great painter, he wrote a long letter in praise of Duveneck's Art, and posted it to New York. He had no acknowledgment from the American Art News, and never saw the letter again: but three years afterwards he received, from Cincinnati, a note announcing a proposed memorial to Duveneck, who had died in the interval. The writer said that the family and friends of the painter had never forgotten the generous and courageous defence of his work offered by Mr. Thomson in reply to his detractors. My old friend continued this narrative by telling me that, in one of the galleries at Venice, he and Mrs. Thomson had seen, many years before, a man making a copy of an angel in one of Titian's pictures, and Mrs. Thomson had said enthusiastically, "Look, what a fine copy it is; it is better than the original!" The painter, turning to them, answered, with an American accent and intonation, "I am glad you like it, and I thank you." This was Duveneck—living through the great and sorrowful romance of his youth. He never worked after the romance ended: but he lived forty years more, and saw the work of his youth honoured.

From an early age Mr. Croal Thomson has taken a prominent and an intimate part in the Art life of London. In addition to his connection with the Paris house of Goupil and the London house of Agnew, he edited The Art Journal for a number of years, contributed to The Studio, The Magazine of Art, The Scotsman, The Encyclopædia Britannica, and published The Barbizon School of Painters, The Brothers Maris, Corot, and numerous other important works.

LORD ARMISTEAD

MR. HENRY GLADSTONE asked me to paint two portraits of Lord Armitstead, his father's old friend. It was during the first winter of the war that the work was carried out.

I found the picturesque invalid reclining in a chair in one of the upper rooms of the house, where he spent the whole day in reading, and seeing now and then his friends. Lord Armitstead was a tall man of striking appearance. His hair and beard were white and long, his face handsome, and his profile marked and finely drawn. His interest in everything that was going on was still eager and at times intense, and although he was supposed to be reading while I painted, the greater part of each sitting was taken up by conversation, which displayed not only great strength of mind, but the rare generosity of recognizing past errors in his own political views and theories, admitting frankly that events then ensuing were not at all in consonance with his long-cherished aspirations. It seemed to delight him to imagine the mind of Mr. Gladstone, whose thoughts he had absorbed during so many years of friendly association, contemplating through his own, as a kind of reflex, the surprising progress of the Liberal Party in the direction of State Socialism, and he often declared that had Mr. Gladstone lived, he would have strongly disapproved of the Radical tendencies of the day. He foreshadowed, with a foresight of the deepest significance, the disruption of the old Liberal Party. He looked like an ancient Druid foretelling, with the inspiration of an oracle, the coming disaster to the Liberal cause.

Of Parliament he hardly spoke save in accents of misgiving and despair; and he did not hesitate to say that since the time he had been a member of the Commons, the whole atmosphere of the House had changed for the worse; that in its present condition he could not have retained a seat in it; that its appearance, as well as its manners and procedure, had completely degenerated. But it was the total disregard of the old form and ceremony that particularly shocked him.

He followed the campaigns in France and on the then victorious Russian front with almost boyish ardour: and the operations in the Dardanelles and in Gallipoli led him to anticipate the capture of Constantinople, and the consequent junction with the Russian armies, with enthusiastic hope.

One morning, when the news from the East seemed to be particularly favourable, he told me that Lord and Lady Morley were coming to lunch; but as Lady Morley was not very well, Lord Morley might come alone. "In that case," he continued, "you may take her place, as there is room at the table for three only." Presently Lord Morley came in alone, and I was introduced to him. He did not remember meeting me at Hawarden many years before, and I found him looking thin and older. I carried on my work until lunch was served. We had it at a small table brought into the room each day. Lord Armitstead took his usual seat, and placed Lord Morley and myself side by side opposite him. The talk was of the war. Presently I turned to Lord Morley and said, "It surprises me that the United States has not yet declared war on Germany." Turning round to face me, with an expression of disdain and in an acrimonious tone, he replied, "Oh, I see! Having got into a mess yourself, you want some one else to pull you out." He had taken me for an Englishman. I did not enlighten him, and from that time addressed myself to the cutlets, which were excellent. A gourmand may not hear what is going on around him, but a gourmet can keep his ears open. Presently Lord Armitstead said, "I see that we shall soon turn the Turks out of Constantinople." Looking up from my plate in time, I saw Lord Morley's thin-cut profile reach across the table almost into Lord Armitstead's flowing white beard, and his acrid voice hissed out, "Yes! and let the Russians in." There are times when the emotions of men seem to burst through their bony barriers, and like waves sweep over you, carrying with them the flotsam and jetsam of a whole fleet of thoughts suddenly struck by a cyclone. I sat overwhelmed, awed by the silence of our host, who seemed to be whispering in his beard, while Lord Morley cynically crunched a bone.

* * * * *

The room in which the invalid sat was heated up to 90°. He did not feel the heat, for his blood circulated slowly; but I suffered, and would often leave the house, mopping my face and head, to enter a cold gray fog full of moist flakes of snow falling slowly and chilling me to the bone. A sudden drop of 55° in the temperature was dangerous, so I hit upon the only safe expedient—for the inside of a cab would have been fatal—which was to run as fast as I could around the corner to Rumpelmeyer's tea-rooms and drink pints of tea so hot that it burnt the mouth. Portrait painting may become a dangerous pastime.

The long sittings with Lord Armitstead for the two portraits were extended to enable me to paint a third for Andrew Carnegie, one of his near friends; but by the time it was completed Mr. Carnegie was also stricken with the infirmities of age, and never saw it. It is the one reproduced.

Lord Armitstead was a willing and capable sitter, making every circumstance easy for the painter, and enlivening the hours with personal anecdotes and reminiscences. Although he had been educated in Germany, and had lived often in that country, he had not been misled into any feeling of sympathy with the people; and he condemned, in the strongest terms, their methods of warfare. He expressed a real sorrow for the loss of so many young men, and particularly for the death of young William Gladstone, of Hawarden. He censured unhesitatingly the War Office for having permitted this brilliant and useful young member of Parliament to enter the fighting line, maintaining, and with sound sense, I thought, that such a man should have been protected by a Staff appointment, because so few young men of his antecedents and capacity could be found to carry on the duties of civil service in times of peace, while there were other young warriors to be had in thousands. I had heard of his death while in America with a feeling of deep regret based upon similar grounds to those put forward by Lord Armitstead.

CYRUS K. CURTIS

AS the clock in the tower of Independence Hall struck the hour of three, a small man took a very large and shapely cigar from his pocket and began to smoke it. With an inimitable twinkle in his right eye, he said to me, as I stood in front of my canvas trying to paint his portrait, "It is time to smoke." As the pale brown cigar changed its tip to a tender gray, and the smoke curled slowly upwards, Mr. Curtis seemed to settle himself more comfortably into the arm-chair that was perched upon a high throne in the corner of the room.

But he was not at his ease. He sat well enough, as regards keeping still in the right position, but I began to notice that he did not belong to the chair, and that discovery was soon followed by the idea that he did not seem to belong to anything, that he was an être apart, self-centred and detached.

Here then was a man with everything which men desire within his reach, at his feet, who possessed one thing only—his mind; all else was immaterial, meaning it was only material and did not matter. And yet it was difficult to believe that such keen eyes allowed the slightest detail to escape their comprehensive gaze.

On mentioning this peculiarity to Mr. Ludington, he showed a little surprise, and almost instantly said, "You should see him on his yacht; he belongs to that!" Here then was the key to Mr. Curtis's character. The yacht moved, it sped through the water, it rose and fell and rolled, and pitched and tossed, and his restless spirit tossed with it. If it anchored in a perfect calm, the harmonious spell would at once be broken, and yacht and man drift asunder.

And then, pursuing the same thought, I pictured the man saying to himself, "What is to be done?" and not "What is to be won?" All things are a means to an end, and the true end is use and not possession. However strong may have been the desire to possess things in the beginning of his career, that feeling had faded before the constantly increasing ambition to achieve something worthy of the admiration, first of himself—that which his own conscience approved—and after himself of his fellow-men. To accumulate and store away riches in the vaults of trust companies would have been, in his case, hiding a very bright light under a bushel. He wanted to see his talent grow and take on the form of architecture, into which he could see worked the handicraft of artisans in wood and stone and mosaics. And he was content to blend his ideas with those of the past, and to follow tradition in form and colour, in order that his neighbours might not be shocked by the violence of contrasts, but soothed and pleased under the spell of harmonious effects.

CHARLES LUDINGTON

MANY years ago, at Costa Lupara, in Alassio, I made a drawing of the young daughter of one of the visitors. Her expression seemed at the same time to penetrate the future, to recall the past, and to contemplate herself with a pathetic sadness. The look revealed itself in the drawing, if anything, more intensely than it did in the girl herself.

A stupid maid, with a dust-brush, whisked out the sketch, and it never could be retrieved.

When I went up to Mount Desert Island, on the coast of Maine, to paint Mr. Ludington, I now and then caught an expression in his face that was unlike that of other men, and I instantly decided that the portrait would not be successful unless this personal look could be obtained. Mr. Ludington had other expressions, more in harmony with everyday events, any one of which might have been delineated with much more certainty and security than this fleeting vision of an inner life.

After enjoying a few gay and happy days in the seaside village, full of young people bent upon sport and merriment, I settled down to work. First making a careful drawing, I began to paint. The work went on almost mechanically for a few hours, when Mrs. Ludington came in and sat down in front of the canvas, on which now was an almost finished head. After a minute or two of silence, she said, "I wonder if you know what you have here?"

For the first time I rose from my chair, to stand off and see from a distance what had been done. To my great delight, the look I wanted had come into the face. It had come unbidden, unsought, without any effort of mine to produce it.

Through long years of experience I have learned to believe that a perfect sitter is nearly a perfect man. It is a test of many qualities, of which goodwill is not the least, and patience and endurance not the best. When I have measured great men by this high standard, it is surprising how really few have been found wanting. But there have been some so disregardful of goodwill that they can only be considered as selfish churls.

Of all the men I have painted, that one whose motto should be suaviter in modo, fortiter in re is Charles Ludington. No one has ever seemed to be just as uniformly gentle or so relentlessly firm as he.

When generous and kindly acts are performed with grace and charm, even a higher feeling than gratitude inspires and elevates the mind. When I recall the great taste displayed by Mr. Ludington in the selection of some fine specimens of old Chinese portraits for the decoration of the panels in his room in the Curtis Building, then the secret link that binds men together in common sympathies begins to reveal itself.

LORD HALIFAX

AT the time of the debate in the House of Lords on the third reading of the Divorce Bill, I was very much interested in the argument of Lord Halifax against the passage of the Bill, and of his final earnest and pathetic appeal to their lordships' House to refuse to give sanction to a measure that was intended to increase the facilities for the commission of what is held to be a sacrilege on any ground but one. "This is probably the last time," said the octogenarian peer, "that I shall ever address your lordships," and, like Chatham when protesting against the separation of the colonies from the Crown, Lord Halifax succumbed to age and weakness, and was carried from the House in an exhausted state.

I did not then think that a few months afterwards my ever-thoughtful friend, Mrs. Drew, would suggest to Lord Halifax that, during his convalescence from an operation for cataract, he might have his portrait painted by me.

When Mrs. Drew told me that I should be expected with my brushes and paints on a certain day, I expressed my pleasure at having the opportunity of meeting such a champion of the sanctity of marriage. My sympathy had always gone out to Josephine because Napoleon had divorced her on such shallow grounds. Had he adopted an heir, as the Roman emperors were not seldom accustomed to do, he very possibly might have saved the Empress from the most humiliating suffering a woman can undergo. When Napoleon took Marie-Louise of Austria to wife, one cannot escape from the thought that he, like Cæsar, allowed social distinction to flower in the field of his amours.

Lord Halifax is a many-sided man of great charm. He was chosen at Oxford, with Mr. W. H. Gladstone, to accompany the Prince of Wales on his first tour of the Continent, in 1857.

Religion is his overmastering passion. As President of the English Church Union, his lifelong passionate desire is the union of the three branches of the Catholic Church—Roman, Anglican, and Greek. It is a significant fact in this age that a host of earnest men of various schools of thought, and from widely different points of view—from that of Lord Halifax and each other—are possessed with this passionate desire for the union of Christendom.

To while away the time as I painted, Mrs. Drew read to us from a character sketch she had written on a statesman of her own day. At Hawarden in 1870, a great friendship had sprung up between members of the Gladstone, Lyttelton, and Balfour families, then meeting for the first time. I gathered that this intimate and exclusive little group of friends was really the nucleus, from 1870 to 1880, of the much larger group of the 'eighties and 'nineties, eventually known as the "souls."

These séances were in every way delightful. The readings freed both the painter and the sitter from the obligation of talking to each other. The light was diffused evenly in a spacious and lofty room from an unusually wide and high window; each one was entertained without the cost of an effort.

There is no weak sentimentalism about the religion of Lord Halifax. He faces the facts of life boldly and fearlessly, and he separates, with an unerring instinct, right from wrong and good from bad.

WALTER TYNDALE

WALTER TYNDALE was fortunate in being born in Bruges—"Bruges la Morte," as Fogazzaro calls it in his romance, Il Santo. Descended from that noble martyr of Tyne-dale, the translator of the Bible, the young Anglo-Fleming was brought up in a babel of strange tongues that found an easy entrance to ears attuned by heredity to the analysis of sounds—many sounds but with one meaning.

In addition to his mother-tongue, he soon babbled in French, Flemish, Walloon, Dutch, German, and the many patois of the districts around his native place, and in after years easily acquired, by a little study and much travel, a knowledge of most of the languages of Europe and some of those of the Orient.

I met him first in Antwerp, at the Royal Academy of Arts. A slender, handsome youth, with very dark hair and eyes, and a complexion that suggested Italian rather than northern origin. Here, under the tuition of De Keyser, Van Lerius, a pupil of Baron Leys, and Buffeau, we worked together with several other English students in the life class, and in idle hours made excursions to the meadows and fields around the Scheldt, or drank lervers and ate smearbrod in the estaminets of the environs of the city. Or, going farther afield, we wandered as far—and the distances are short in the Low Countries—as Malines and Brussels, or northward to Rotterdam, The Hague, Haarlem, and Amsterdam, to study the masterpieces of Dutch and Flemish Art, in private as well as public galleries. It was at this time that the portraits by Franz Hals were revealed to me in that little museum in Haarlem; and although I was inclined then to admire the Syndics by Rembrandt, I soon discovered, by frequent visits to Haarlem and close study of the painting, in the groups of burghers by Hals, in the purity and freshness of his colour, and the consummate skill displayed in the handling, in the deftness of touch and the accuracy of form, that the mastery lay with Hals and not with Rembrandt. Frequent pilgrimages to that Mecca of portraiture over a period of nearly fifty years has only tended to convince me of the correctness of an early judgment.

We young, ambitious, and hopeful aspirants to fame were rather inclined to look upon the bituminous colours of the old canvases with questioning eyes, for the crudities of nature appealed strongly to senses that had not yet learned to discriminate between nature chaste and nature prurient, and Art was then entering upon the period that has ended with the cult of the ugly and the worship of the commonplace and the abnormal.

We could not believe that the Rembrandts and Franz Hals and Ver Meers were just as fresh in colour when they left the easels as nature seems to be, and that time and dust and varnish had given that warmth and glow of colour that we called vieux jeu. We were not revolutionaries, we were simply ignoramuses. We were not wicked, but we were also not virtuosi.

After a separation that lasted about two years, Tyndale and I met again in London, and here we also renewed friendships with other students of the academy in Antwerp.

The first time I painted Walter Tyndale he posed as a courtier, in a dress of the period of George III, for a picture called Tubbing the Prince, an imitation of the Spanish School of Zamacois and Fortuny, then very much the vogue, because of the brilliancy of the technique, and the cleverness of the characterization of bygone types. This school comprised the French painter Boldini, one of the greatest adepts in the handling of a brush, either on a small or large scale, that has ever graced an atelier. One of his masterpieces is a portrait of Whistler, in the Brooklyn art gallery, by far the most characteristic likeness of that eccentric master.

It was during these sittings that Tyndale gave me that our divergencies of views upon political and social questions developed. Although we agreed upon other matters, we disagreed fundamentally upon the Irish question, the trade union, and in general the Radical movements of the day. Walter Tyndale is not a Socialist, as so many artists are, or pretend to be. There is nothing of the William Morris or Walter Crane in his constitution. He espoused the causes that the Radicals and the great Liberal statesmen were conscientiously working for, and he believed he could see in the success of Liberalism a regeneration of the people. I was not so optimistic, and I foreboded many dire calamities to the nation, through the ambitions of Labour leaders. I frankly admit that he seemed to have the charitable, the generous, and the neighbourly point of view; but I was held by certain inalienable principles which, however sternly individualist they may appear to be, always move along certain well-defined lines to a goal; and that goal is the stability of civilization.

To me certain truisms are to be deduced from an intelligent study of history and through just observation of present conditions. One is that the strength of a community is measured by the strength of its strongest member and not by the weakest. This test is the direct opposite of that applied to a plank or to a chain, whose strength is that of its weakest link or its greatest flaw. Another is that to increase the power of the strong is a better safeguard to a nation than to attempt to strengthen the weak, for there are innate defects in the weak that cannot be cured. In reformers there is always a disposition to criticize the strong just because they are strong. The Socialists, of course, deny them the right of strength, arguing that because some are weak all should be weak, or at least of an equal strength.

And so we fought our battles, in the Gray House, that house of mystery, in Hornton Street at the corner of the Abbey Mews, in Alpha House, in Murestead, and at last in The Hermitage, prior to and after 1914, when my oft-repeated prophetic warnings concerning the intentions of the German peoples have come true. In time of war have the police the right to open a road that the military has closed? This was one of the questions warmly disputed between us.

Under this trifling matter there is a principle that pierces as a sword to the foundation of society. In the last resort the soldier rules, and always will rule.

But the great problem of the inequalities among men was worthy of our attention as a subject becoming ever more important as humanity grows and groans under the weight of its possessions.

Both of us were well informed upon the scale that differentiated the labourer with fifty pounds a year from the manufacturer earning, by the employment of labourers, from ten to one hundred or more thousands a year; or between a parson with a dozen children and a stipend of eighty to one hundred and fifty pounds a year from a Carnegie, with one child and millions a year. These things worried George Meredith in his late years. He wrote letters about them, and he talked to me about them at Box Hill, where I went to make studies for his portrait. They worry everybody save the selfish rich.

But these extremes, it may be said, are no worse than they have always been, excepting in one respect—the taste to expend. It is absurd to blame the strong, i.e. the wealthy, merely because they are strong. Where they are open to criticism is the way they use their strength, or chiefly because they hoard it. A man who does not keep a yacht or a racing stable can live luxuriously on from two to five thousand pounds a year. If he has twenty or thirty thousand a year and invests the balance in stocks and shares, instead of spending it tastefully, he is a hoarder, if not a miser, and is not doing half his duty to his community. There is where I differ from most of the Radicals, for no one admires strength and inequality more than I do.

The inequalities in the universe make it go round instead of flying apart, hold it together instead of disintegrating it. A few fools and many rogues think equality would be heavenly, but it would be deadly dull.

Walter Tyndale soon became fascinated with the East, where he was obliged to pass the winters in order to escape the injurious effects upon his health of the coal-smoke of London. Here his tastes for the beauty of contours and of rich colour found expression in a series of charming watercolour drawings of scenes in Japan, India, Egypt, and Italy. But drawing alone did not suffice as an outlet for his enthusiastic admiration for the mosque and the Moslem. He was at last inspired to use a literary gift that had been as a talent lying hidden in a napkin. The result has been the publication of a number of admirable books upon Egypt, Japan, and Italy, all illustrated in a masterly way by his own brush.

At the outbreak of the war the Government discovered his proficiency in European languages, and appointed him chief censor at Boulogne, where he remained until the armistice was signed.

JOHN MALCOLM SWAN

JOHN SWAN stands in a niche by himself. His Art is precious, like a jewel, to be handled lovingly in the seclusion of a cabinet of treasures, not exposed to the vulgar in the glare and blare of artificiality for ostentation's sake.

He loved Art for its cunning and its craft, and with deft and skilful fingers lingered long over the making of it, full of the joy of creating. At times he could be swift and impress movement and thought upon paper with a magic stroke of his crayon or chalk. Just as Manet and Monet sought for light, Swan aimed for movement, watching always for feline grace and charm in the animals that can purr as well as scream and bite.

The suppleness of the cat tribe roused in him every artistic instinct, and Barye himself has not translated into bronze or stone the majestic poise of the kings of the jungle with more intuitive skill.

His line is full of serpent-like undulations, breaking, disappearing, blurring; it is played upon as a chord in music is vibrated subtly by the musician who moves you. Line is to drawing what a strophe is to music, a phrase to prose, rhythm to poetry—it is God-given and never acquired.

Swan was a fine draughtsman, in the best sense, for his very imperfections were full of unconscious beauty. There is nothing more unpleasant than good drawing, so-called, which sweeps around a contour unerringly like a rigid wire, moved by a mechanical spirit that repels imagination. It is comparable only to a portrait that looks as if the epidermis had been removed. Before such an image one can only say, "This is a man with the bloom rubbed off." Why emulate a technique that only Van Eyck has mastered? In his really miraculous painting in the National Gallery, John Arnolfini and his Wife, the fine art lies in the face of the man, shadowed under the great hat; all the rest is just perfect mechanism and inimitable.

There are but few artists who have had tactful fingers—Rodin Whistler, Swan, Zorn. Many have had a bold fist, as Swan called it; the greatest of these is Peter Paul Rubens, that Prince of Painters whose comprehensive sweep includes all styles, all subjects, and whose achievement cannot be estimated or measured.

Swan was one of a trio of true artists, one of three minds bent upon the same ideal, the only ideal because it is the true, because it is Nature. He was happy in his friends. In Alfred Gilbert he found the bold and aspiring genius; in Onslow Ford the gentle and tender artist; and in a shrine of his own, a recluse in the hidden glades of the classic resort of the muse, there was that mysterious oracle, Matthew Maris, with whom he often sought to commune.

Swan was absent-minded, or perhaps it would be more correct to say, since his work was always uppermost in his thoughts, that he was present-minded. He took no count of time. I have never seen him look at a watch, and, like myself, he perhaps never carried one.

He would come in the morning to make me "a short call," stay on for lunch, linger over a cigar and glass of port until tea steamed in the pot, forget himself in the mazes of an abstract theory until dinner was served, be deaf to the stroke of midnight, and at last, as the clock struck two, slowly and reluctantly descend the steps to the garden and the outer door, ending his argument with a "Do you follow me?" to which I would yawningly reply, "No, I am going to bed."

SIR ARCHIBALD GEIKIE

WHILE visiting Walter Tyndale, in Haslemere, he suggested that I should take advantage of the proximity of the President of the Royal Society, Sir Archibald Geikie, and make a portrait of him.

Sir Archibald gave me the whole day between breakfast and tea for the sittings. He did not take luncheon, for he had found that the day was broken in two by a useless and injurious meal, that after lunching the mind was in no condition for work because the body became torpid and dormant, and required repose. He maintained better health and accomplished more work by eating a good breakfast early in the morning, a good tea at four o'clock, and a substantial dinner at seven o'clock. Lord Leighton had adopted the same custom, with equally beneficial results.

I had the advantage of long sittings, which enabled me to complete the portrait very quickly. If I happened to be hungry, the Tyndales' house was next door, where Mrs. Tyndale always welcomed me. Sir Archibald and I were in complete agreement upon philosophical, political, and social questions, so that we found much pleasure in attacking the weak points in the flimsy armour of imaginary opponents. Sir Archibald, like John Tyndall, was a doughty champion of the truth that he had found in rocky mountains, in sandy valleys, and in fossils deep down in the strata of the earth—truth that had often exposed the aberrations of the mind of man, for, as he would no doubt have admitted had I put the matter before him, the only false thing on earth is man. Some few animals, like the fox and the spider and the dove, know how to deceive, but as a rule Nature does not lie.

But there was one subject broached which almost caused a serious rupture between Sir Archibald and myself. I had been asked to dinner to meet a few of his friends. During the repast the little fairies who buzz around to create mischief for their own amusement put it into my head to mention Bacon in connection with Shakespeare, when in an instant Sir Archibald turned very pink, and angrily declared that he would not have that heresy mentioned in his house, that it was a monstrous and disloyal thing to give tongue or ear to anything so detrimental to the honour of English traditions. I murmured a regret; but that, instead of appeasing him, seemed to irritate him the more until a frosty and still atmosphere settled over the table, and I thought we were all going to shrivel up. At last some tactful guest broke through the ice, and when a little wine had restored the circulation we settled down to the chicken and bacon, and concluded to swallow both Stratford-on-Avon and Verulam.

SIR HENRY IRVING

AT the time that Irving was giving sittings to Onslow Ford, for the Hamlet, I often met the great actor: and at one of these meetings it was suggested that I should make a drawing of him similar to a pastel I had made of Ford. Irving asked me to come to the Lyceum Theatre and draw him in his dressing-room. For some reason the drawing proceeded badly, and I had to discard the first attempt and begin a second. When it was well advanced, Irving went behind me and, looking over my shoulder for a minute without saying a word, crossed to the door leading down to the stage and called, "Bram! Come here!" In a minute Bram Stoker appeared, and Irving, who was standing behind me, said to him, "Who does that look like?"

"Moses in the city," replied Bram.

Irving's impersonation of Shylock was admirable. I liked him better as Becket; and he could have played Macbeth if he had not misread the intention of the play. To him Macbeth was a poetic villain from birth; and he once, I believe, wrote a magazine article to show that he was right in that interpretation of the thane's character. Lewis Campbell, of St. Andrews, did not agree with him.

I can well remember going to the Lyceum to see his Macbeth. When he appeared on the stage, his expression, attitude, and demeanour indicated so truly the scoundrel, that I wondered how Duncan could address him as "worthy," and I turned to my wife and said, "He takes Macbeth to be a rogue from the first," and that notion was so much in dissonance to my own that the night's entertainment was spoiled for me, and I never saw him again in the rôle.

The play becomes utterly commonplace and meaningless if the assumption be made that Macbeth is an ordinary criminal. What becomes of the witches' prophecies, the wife's "screwing up your courage to the sticking point," the hesitation of the tender-hearted but ambitious Cawdor, the cowardly remorse, followed by the recklessness of despair? All these subtleties were thrown away on a man really bad, and fearless of the consequences of his misdeeds—or was he just trying to fool himself and all the others by pretending to be tempted by ambition, by soothsayers, and a relentlessly ambitious woman?

If the play is not intended to show by degrees how a brave, superstitious, and ambitious man of honourable character can be led astray by occult warnings of the inevitableness of destiny, by the taunts of a contemptuous wife, and by the spurrings of a vaulting ambition, then it was written to small purpose.

The author clearly intended to depict the wavering moods of a weak mind in a brave body, tortured by temptation. To make Macbeth's villainy innate and premeditated is equalled by the attempt of Mrs. Stille of Philadelphia to show that Lady Macbeth is a much misunderstood and maligned woman, whose chief fault lay in her over-devotion to a weak and wicked husband.

When I questioned Irving about his reading of Macbeth, he explained his views without convincing me of their merit.

Ellen Terry was in disagreement with both Coquelin aîné and Irving on the question of "feeling a part." The two latter claimed that the best results were obtained by a cold reasoning performance of a part, while Ellen Terry maintained that anger must be real anger, hate real hate, and love real love.

If she were really mad as Ophelia or Lady Macbeth, it is just as well that the madness is only assumed for the moment. That most polished actor, Coquelin, not only did not feel the passion of his part, but he conveyed no emotion to his hearers, save admiration for his technical skill: laughter might be evoked by his mimicry, but tears refused to flow at the sight of his misfortunes. Tact is the great artist, in life as in music, or in painting or sculpture, or architecture. He who touches you wins your sympathy, even though his handling be not quite perfect.

Sargent, in his painted story of the religions, excites no religious emotion, but Thouron does in the Flaming Heart.

One other point about Irving—was he a great artist despite his mannerisms, or partly because of them? An actor without mannerisms is like a musician without hair. Irving may have assumed his peculiar gait and speech, just as Puvis de Chavannes divested his designs of academic forms and replaced them by archaic inaccuracies, to impress, not only the people, but the connoisseurs. The hero of a drama or a tragedy is not expected to be a conventional or commonplace character, unless Ibsen creates him. There is an extreme range and variety of personalities in Shakespeare's plays, but they are all marked men. If Irving had invented a change in mannerism—one for Lear, one for Becket, and one for Macbeth—he would have freed himself from the criticism of the objectors. But his speech and his gait betrayed his own personality showing through the disguise, and that was his sign-manual and seal of nobility. Without his mannerisms there would not have been the touch of Irving, and by his tact he was greater than the greatest actor of his day.

THE PORTRAIT I DID NOT PAINT

ONE summer as I was on the point of sailing for America I received, by cablegram, a commission to paint, for the Catholics of Philadelphia, a portrait of the Pope. As to the character of the portrait I was given carte blanche.

Here was an opportunity that I had not even imagined—to paint the most spiritual in appearance and ethereal personage of his day, or perhaps of any day. The Pope had often been described to me, when borne aloft in procession through St. Peter's on great festival occasions, as appearing to be unreal, immaterial, so pale and transparent and pure was his countenance, opalescent in its radiance, and illumined by a slight smile in the corners of a mouth whose firm lines betrayed the inner consciousness of a great responsibility. A fondness for the pearly gray tints of life, for the pastel-like quality of surfaces, led me to look upon this commission as the culminating episode of a fortunate career, and that if only a mere suggestion of the spiritual beauty of the pontiff could be attained I might consider that I had not painted in vain. Many of my friends congratulated me on my good fortune in being asked to paint a subject so completely in sympathy with my favourite scheme of colour, and I was happy in the thought that the portrait was destined for my native city, where I was already represented by one of Mr. Gladstone. But l'homme propose et Dieu dispose. No amount of free will on my part could shake the inevitable rock of predestination, and the picture still remains in my imagination, a much more beautiful thing than it could have been on canvas.

No effort had been made to obtain sittings for me; that was left entirely to my own initiative. I expected there would be difficulties to overcome, but with such a goal for ambition, hope easily overcame them in advance. Several good people suggested good advice, but no one was willing to risk his amour propre, and when Onslow Ford, who was doing the portrait of the Duke of Norfolk, an amiable man of great goodwill, received a courteous note from His Grace to say that he could not interfere in so delicate a matter, I was aroused to the serious nature of the obstacles I should have to overcome. As much time had already been wasted in correspondence and interviews, I decided to go to Rome and take the bull by the horns.

Starting off with my wife, we first lingered in the inspiring atmosphere of Paris, and then hastened to Florence, where we greeted many old friends, and thence to Rome. It had been suggested that the head of the American College in Rome could assist me. Not wishing to waste any more time, I applied to the College, and while waiting for the reply from its Rector, went to the British Embassy and saw Sir Clare Ford, who greeted me with "Why do you come to me? You should go to the American Minister. So you want to paint the Pope, do you? Well, I'll bet you three hundred dollars you won't." I replied that I had come to him because he could help me, or suggest something, and that as I was an old resident of London and a ratepayer in two counties in England, I thought I could claim his aid and indulgence. This seemed to have some effect upon him, and being an offhand sort of man, and not standing too strictly on the dignity of his high office, he sat down cosily beside me and continued, "You will not be received at the Vatican for any such purpose; the Pope is old and ill, and any time he has to spare has to be given to his ecclesiastical duties. You can obtain an audience as other strangers do, but as for anything else, make up your mind now that all your efforts will be futile. Why, they will treat you just like a carpenter or any other workman. Artists are nothing to them. Life is a serious matter to the Church."

"They must be very different from the old popes, then," I replied, "for they loved to honour and to patronize artists and Art. Have they changed so much as that? "I don't know if they have changed," Sir Clare began, but I interrupted him, for I was beginning to be nettled, by warmly saying, "I have no doubt that Michael Angelo was a very good carpenter, as well as architect and sculptor and poet, and that Giotto and Leonardo da Vinci and Cellini were all good workmen, as well as great geniuses. Where would the Church be now if it had not been for these men who have given it substantial and material evidence of greatness? Is not St. Peter's the glory of the Church, and did not Michael Angelo design it? Is not the Vatican, with all its treasures, the work of artists, and is it not the home of the popes?"

"Oh! tut, tut!" broke in the Ambassador, "the Pope would be just as great and just as much sought after and worshipped if he lived under a tent in the desert." Then changing the subject, as he thought, he asked me how long I had been in Rome and if I were alone. On telling him I had brought my wife, he said, "You should take her about, especially if she has not been here before. This is an interesting place; there is much to be seen in ancient as well as modern monuments. People flock here to see the remains of the great Roman builders, like the Colosseum, the Baths of Caracalla, the Forum, and other architectural remains, all constituting the chief glory of the Roman emperors, and, of course, the later period, when the Church was aiming at supremacy over the civil power, and at the height of its glory and splendour devoted its great wealth and influence to the creation of the Vatican, St. Peter's, and the many other churches."

Listening until he had finished, I rose, thanked him for his kind reception and courtesy, and departed, wondering.

Finding no encouragement here, I attacked the Vatican, and wasted days in marching up and down its marble stairs, until the guards and huissiers must have wondered what I was so persistent in seeking. At last one of the ecclesiastics to whom I had been directed, who held some official position in the offices of the Vatican, and whose name I now forget, awakened in me such a sense of indignation that I expostulated with him in tones that brought him to a more obliging disposition of mind, and he advised me to see Cardinal Rampollo, who was in a position to grant or refuse my request at once. He could have told me this before. After he had listened to my criticisms of the Church's attitude in living upon the past and doing nothing for the present or the future of Art, and was convinced that Rome had passed through three successive periods—of greatness, under the Cæsars, of mediocrity, under the popes, and of decadence, under the modern kings—by referring him to the architecture of each period to

JOHN McLURE HAMILTON
(By Onslow Ford)

corroborate rate my statements, he changed his manner of indifference to one of attention and became, in the end, polite.

I obtained the promise of a reception by Cardinal Rampollo. On the day appointed I mounted a long flight of steps to the top of the Vatican and was ushered into a room richly furnished in gold and brocade. In a few minutes the Cardinal entered. He greeted me simply and kindly, and pointing to one corner of a high-backed gilt sofa, in the rococo style, he seated himself close to me in the other. We might have known each other all our lives. His easy and restful poise, his affable speech, led me to suppose that he was prepared for a friendly talk of any length and that affairs of State could wait.

"I am sorry that His Holiness cannot be approached upon the subject of having his portrait painted," was his ultimatum. "He is not well, is, as you know, old and weak; besides, he does not give sittings for the portraits that are painted of him." I reminded him that two French painters, Benjamin

Constant and Chartran, had painted large portraits of the Pope that had been exhibited in the Salon and elsewhere, and that newspapers had printed long accounts of their interviews with the Pope and the sittings that had been accorded by him. Leaning forward towards me, and contracting his dark brows over his piercing coal-black eyes, he said earnestly, "Do you suppose that an artist, with his easel, his palette and brushes, and all his paraphernalia, could come here and enter the presence of the Holy Father without my knowledge? I am near him every moment, night and day, and no one approaches him but through me."

"You must believe me or the newspapers," continued the Cardinal, and added, "I think you should know that the Pope has sat for his portrait but once. At the earnest request of a member of the Pecci family, and in the interest of a young man, intimately known to the family, the Pope was persuaded to grant him a few sittings. All the other portraits have been painted from sketches, made, perhaps, during public audiences, from memory, or from photographs."

While His Eminence was talking the thought entered my head to ask him for a sitting. He was princely in appearance, of a dark, strong, southern type, with well-developed features. The long, black frock, touched here and there with purple and gold, the black hair and biretta against the background of gold and damask, made an imposing picture. Had there been a mirror on the other side of the room, reflecting him and me, I should have been shocked at the contrast between our two personalities—one belonging to all time, tall and attired with dignity that welcomes respect, the other clad in jacket and trousers that belong to no time and repel every æsthetic sense, as well as respect.

My disappointment was mollified by what had been recounted to me by this courteous and kindly Prince of the Church, and, saying good-bye, I slowly descended the marble steps, sad but not angry. The dream had vanished. Rome had no further interest for me.

Some time after this, when I visited the International Exhibition in Chicago, I saw in one of the picture galleries the portrait of Leo XIII by the young friend of the Pecci family. It bore upon its face the proof of Cardinal Rampollo's statement that it had been painted from nature.

www.ingramcontent.com/pod-product-compliance
Lightning Source LLC
Chambersburg PA
CBHW051504170526
45166CB00001B/373
* 9 7 8 1 5 2 2 8 4 0 4 3 5 *